Math Tutor: Fractions & Decimals

Author:	Hal Torrance
Editors:	Mary Dieterich and Sarah M. Anderson
Proofreader:	Margaret Brown

COPYRIGHT © 2011 Mark Twain Media, Inc.

ISBN 978-1-58037-574-0

Printing No. CD-404146

Mark Twain Media, Inc., Publishers
Distributed by Carson-Dellosa Publishing LLC

HPS 231527

Table of Contents

How to Use This Book

Each new concept is introduced in a short **Absorb** section. The Absorb section primarily focuses on a single skill or concept. Key terms are highlighted for easy identification. The **Apply** section then gives the student practice in that skill. Each concept is followed by **Extra Practice** pages to give students opportunities for further reinforcement of the skills learned.

Due to the sequential nature of mathematics, this book has been arranged in a systematic way, with each new skill building on those learned previously. For instance, reducing fractions is not presented until after factoring has been covered as a topic. Therefore, students should not attempt to reduce fractions until the fundamental underlying skill of factoring has been introduced. It is recommended to follow the order set out in the book; however, if students need extra practice or review in a certain skill, this book is an excellent resource for tutoring students where they most need help.

The section **Final Review: All Topics** can serve as a good pretest if one is needed for planning a more focused course of study. There are also three different **Section Reviews** that focus on the cumulative skills presented to that point in the book.

Descriptions and suggested uses for each section of this book are listed below:

1. **What Is a Fraction?** is best used with **2. A Basic Fraction Has Two Parts**. These sections reinforce the concept of a fraction and its basic parts. The terms numerator and denominator are not used until the end of this section, once the student has had practice writing fractions used to describe a given situation.

3. **Finding a Common Denominator** reviews the concept of multiples and finding the Least Common Multiple (LCM). Students apply the concept of multiples to finding common denominators for fraction pairs. Since addition and subtraction of fractions are used as examples in this activity, the activity concludes with adding fraction pairs, once the pairs have been changed into equivalents with common denominators.

4. **Adding Fractions** is best used with **5. Subtracting Fractions.** In these sections, simple fractions (no mixed numbers involved) are added and subtracted. Common denominators will need to be found in many of the problems. Students should not try to reduce fractions in this section, since those skills are reviewed in the sections that immediately follow.

6. **Reducing Fractions** reviews the concept of factors and how they relate to reducing fractions.

7. **More About Reducing Fractions** continues practice with reducing fractions to lowest terms. These sections are best used with…

8. **Improper Fractions**, which extends the practice of reducing fractions to mixed numbers. These sections come after students have already worked with adding and subtracting fractions. Moving forward from this section, reducing fractions will be an expected part of all exercises.

Section Review 1 and Section Review 1 Extra Practice review concepts covered to this point.

How to Use This Book (cont.)

9. **Converting Fractions to Decimal Numbers** is best used with **10. Ordering Fractions.** These sections will give students an understanding of the relative sizes of fractions and how decimal equivalents are found. Calculators are recommended for this activity, since the focus should be finding decimal equivalents for fractions and comparing fractions, as opposed to the mechanics of dividing.

11. **Adding Mixed Numbers and Improper Fractions** extends earlier work with adding fractions. A checklist is provided for students to use for approaching addition problems involving mixed numbers and improper fractions.

12. **Subtracting Mixed Numbers and Improper Fractions** extends earlier work with subtracting fractions. A checklist is provided for students to use for approaching subtraction problems involving mixed numbers and improper fractions.

13. **More Practice Adding and Subtracting Fractions** includes additional practice adding and subtracting fractions with a short section on word problems.

    Section Review 2 and Section Review 2 Extra Practice review concepts covered to this point.

14. **Converting Decimals to Fractions** is best used with **15. Converting Fractions to Percents**. These sections build on earlier work where students converted fractions into decimals. Here, however, the process is reversed. A calculator is useful for this activity.

16. **Multiplying Fractions** is best used with **17. Dividing Fractions.** These sections introduce multiplying and dividing basic fractions.

18. **Multiplying Fractions and Mixed Numbers** extends earlier work with multiplying fractions to include mixed numbers and whole numbers. Reducing with common factors is reviewed.

19. **Dividing Fractions and Mixed Numbers** extends earlier work with dividing fractions to include mixed numbers and whole numbers. Reducing with common factors is reviewed.

20. **More Practice Multiplying and Dividing Fractions** includes additional practice in multiplying and dividing fractions with a section on word problems.

    Section Review 3 and Section Review 3 Extra Practice review concepts covered to this point.

    Final Review: All Sections and **Final Review Extra Practice:** Due to its length, this section should be split into two or more different sessions for students. A calculator is recommended. An alternate use for this section would be as a pretest to define areas that need additional attention before beginning the book.

Section 1 — What Is a Fraction?

ABSORB

- • A **fraction** is simply a portion of something.

- • Fractions are used in two basic ways:

A. A fraction can be used for describing part of a single item.

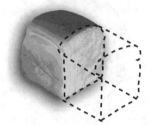

This drawing shows $\frac{1}{2}$ of the loaf of bread is gone.

B. A fraction can be used for describing parts of a group.

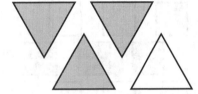

This drawing shows $\frac{3}{4}$ of the triangles are shaded.

In the drawing below, which fraction should correctly describe the shaded portion?

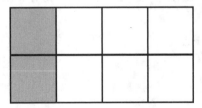

Circle one: $\frac{3}{7}$ $\frac{5}{5}$ $\frac{2}{8}$ $\frac{6}{9}$

$\frac{2}{8}$ is the correct answer.

Name: _____ Date: _____

Section **1** **What Is a Fraction?**

APPLY   Now try a few fractions on your own.

1. In the drawing below, which fraction correctly describes the shaded portion?

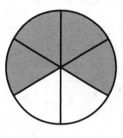

Circle one: $\frac{3}{6}$ $\frac{2}{6}$ $\frac{4}{6}$ $\frac{3}{4}$

2. In the drawing below, which fraction correctly describes the non-shaded portion?

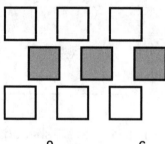

Circle one: $\frac{3}{9}$ $\frac{9}{3}$ $\frac{6}{9}$ $\frac{6}{3}$

3. In the space below, make a drawing to represent the fraction $\frac{4}{5}$.

Name: _____ Date: _____

Section **1** What Is a Fraction?

EXTRA PRACTICE Complete the following exercise.

1. In the drawing below, which fraction correctly describes the shaded portion?

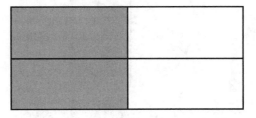

Circle one: $\frac{1}{2}$ $\frac{1}{3}$ $\frac{1}{4}$ $\frac{1}{8}$

2. In the drawing below, which fraction correctly describes the non-shaded portion?

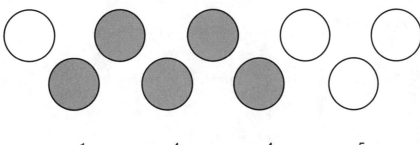

Circle one: $\frac{1}{4}$ $\frac{4}{5}$ $\frac{4}{9}$ $\frac{5}{9}$

3. In the space below, make a drawing to represent the fraction $\frac{5}{6}$.

Name: _____   Date: _____

Section **2** A Basic Fraction Has Two Parts

ABSORB   Look at the circle below that has been split into 6 equal parts. One of the parts has been shaded.

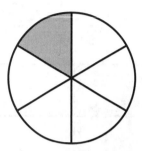

The fraction describing the shaded portion of this circle would be $\frac{1}{6}$. Why is that?

The bottom number of a fraction, in this case 6, always describes the total number of portions involved. The circle has been drawn with six pieces, so the bottom portion of the fraction will be 6.

The top number of a fraction, in this case 1, always describes the number of portions being examined or affected. There is one section shaded out of a total of six sections in the entire circle.

That's why this fraction is written as $\frac{1}{6}$.

APPLY   For each example, write a fraction to express the portion shown.

1.   Dark marbles as a portion of all the marbles. _____

2.   Shaded blocks as a portion of the overall square. _____

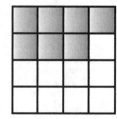

Name: _____ Date: _____

Section ② A Basic Fraction Has Two Parts

3. Striped fish as a portion of the overall school of fish. _____

The following problems are not illustrated, but they work exactly the same way. Think of the overall number and the portion being affected. Write the fraction to describe each situation.

4. _____ Eighty-one students of 405 total students forgot that it was school picture day. Express the portion that forgot.

5. _____ A jar contained exactly 500 coins, of which 367 are pennies. Express the pennies as a portion of the overall jar of coins.

6. _____ Sixteen of the town's 76 firefighters have called in sick during the flu season. Express the portion that have called in sick.

7. _____ A student club has 14 total members. Three of those member got angry during a club meeting and walked out. Express the portion of the club members who did not leave the meeting.

8. _____ A barn held a herd of 8 milk cows. A door was left open, and 5 walked out. Express the portion of the herd that stayed in the barn.

9. _____ Out of a box of 200 toothpicks, there were 44 used during a party. Express the portion that was used during the party.

10. _____ Four out of 17 computers in the computer lab were damaged by a lightning strike outside. Express the portion that was not damaged.

Your teacher may provide you with an answer key. Then, if you missed any, go back and figure out why they were missed.

Now take a look at one more thing about the basic parts of a fraction. The top number in a fraction is called the **numerator**. The bottom number in a fraction is called the **denominator**. At this point, we'll start using those terms when we discuss the parts of a fraction.

$$\frac{\text{Numerator}}{\text{Denominator}}$$

Name: _____   Date: _____

Section [2] A Basic Fraction Has Two Parts

EXTRA PRACTICE   For each example, write a fraction to express the portion shown.

1.   Shaded baseballs as a portion of all the baseballs. _____

2.   Shaded squares as a portion of the overall grid. _____

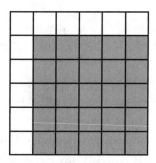

3.   Spotted dogs as portion of all the dogs. _____

4.   Convertibles as a portion of all the cars. _____

Name: _____ Date: _____

Section ② A Basic Fraction Has Two Parts

For each situation below, think of the overall number and then the portion being affected. Write the fraction to describe each situation.

5. _____ Twenty-five students out of a total of 500 did not want to eat the pizza being served for lunch. Express the portion that did not want pizza.

6. _____ A piggy bank held 600 coins, and 457 of those were nickels. Express the nickels as a portion of the overall coins in the bank.

7. _____ Out of a state's 150 cities, 89 have voted to go smoke-free. Express the smoke-free cities as a portion of the total number of cities.

8. _____ Five members of a 25-member club had to leave the meeting early. Express the portion of the club members who did not leave early.

9. _____ There were 35 chickens in a coop, and 15 got loose. Express the chickens that got loose as a portion of the total number of chickens.

10. _____ Out of a package of 300 bamboo skewers, 23 were used. Express the number of unused skewers as a portion of the total number of skewers.

11. _____ Six of the school's 25 computers got infected by a virus. Express the number of infected computers as a portion of the total number of computers.

12. _____ The hospital employs 62 nurses. Twenty-four nurses were on duty for the afternoon shift. Express the number of nurses on duty as a portion of the total number of nurses.

Name: _____ Date: _____

Section **3** Finding a Common Denominator

ABSORB

We learned in previous sections that a fraction is used for showing a portion of a single item or a portion of a group. We also learned that a fraction is composed of a top number, the numerator, and a bottom number, the denominator.

Before we can add or subtract fractions, the denominators must be the same. Sometimes fractions that need to be added or subtracted will already come with like denominators. Often, the denominators will first need to be changed in order to add or subtract the fractions.

Getting some practice with multiples will give us the background we need for finding a common denominator. So we'll set the notion of fractions aside for a moment and concentrate on multiples.

Here's an example of the multiples of the number 4:

4, 8, 12, 16, 20, 24, 28, 32, 36, 40, 44, 48

No doubt you recognized these from your multiplication tables.

Now, let's look at the multiples of another number, 8:

8, 16, 24, 32, 40, 48, 56, 64, 72, 80, 88, 96

We can look at both lists and tell that some of these multiples are the same; 4 and 8 share some common multiples. In fact, 8 is itself a multiple of 4. In this example, 8 would be the **Least Common Multiple** (LCM) of the two numbers.

APPLY

Find the first ten multiples for each number.

1. 3 _____

2. 7 _____

3. 10 _____

Now find the Least Common Multiple for each pair of numbers.

4. 5, 20 _____   **5.** 6, 8 _____

6. 3, 7 _____   **7.** 4, 18 _____

Section 3 | Finding a Common Denominator

ABSORB   As mentioned earlier, finding a common denominator is a first step before adding or subtracting fractions.

Steps to go through in order to find a common denominator:

A.   Determine if one denominator is a multiple of the other. If we need to find a common denominator for the fractions $\frac{1}{3}$ and $\frac{1}{12}$, it's pretty clear that 12 is a multiple of 3. In fact 3 x 4 = 12, so our multiplier for changing $\frac{1}{3}$ to some number of 12ths would be 4.

In this case, $\frac{1}{3}$ would become $\frac{4}{12}$, once both numerator and denominator have been multiplied by 4. So $\frac{4}{12}$ is the equivalent fraction for $\frac{1}{3}$.

Now we could take $\frac{4}{12}$ and $\frac{1}{12}$ and do something with these fractions, such as:

add them: $\frac{4}{12} + \frac{1}{12} = \frac{5}{12}$ or subtract them: $\frac{4}{12} - \frac{1}{12} = \frac{3}{12}$

B.   In many cases, one denominator is not a multiple of the other. We then have to find a common denominator based on the least common multiple. For instance, consider the fractions $\frac{2}{3}$ and $\frac{1}{7}$.

21 is the least common multiple of 3 and 7. So both fractions have to be changed to some amount of 21sts.

To get $\frac{2}{3}$ into some amount of 21sts, the multiplier is 7. So $\frac{2}{3}$ will become $\frac{14}{21}$, once both numerator and denominator are multiplied by 7.

To get $\frac{1}{7}$ into some amount of 21sts, the multiplier is 3. So $\frac{1}{7}$ will become $\frac{3}{21}$, once both the numerator and denominator are multiplied by 3.

Now we could take these fractions and:

add them: $\frac{14}{21} + \frac{3}{21} = \frac{17}{21}$ or subtract them: $\frac{14}{21} - \frac{3}{21} = \frac{11}{21}$

Name: _____   Date: _____

Section ③ Finding a Common Denominator

APPLY

PART 1
For each pair of fractions, name the Least Common Denominator (LCD).

1. $\frac{7}{8}, \frac{22}{10}$ _____

2. $\frac{2}{5}, \frac{6}{10}$ _____

3. $\frac{3}{6}, \frac{1}{12}$ _____

For each pair of fractions, convert both to equivalent fractions with a Least Common Denominator (LCD) so that the pair could be added or subtracted.

4a. $\frac{2}{3}, \frac{5}{6}$ _____ _____

5a. $\frac{2}{12}, \frac{1}{5}$ _____ _____

6a. $\frac{1}{6}, \frac{3}{8}$ _____ _____

7a. $\frac{2}{14}, \frac{4}{7}$ _____ _____

8a. $\frac{5}{13}, \frac{1}{39}$ _____ _____

9a. $\frac{1}{4}, \frac{1}{16}$ _____ _____

10a. $\frac{3}{4}, \frac{7}{8}$ _____ _____

PART 2
Since you now have the fractions changed into common denominators, go ahead and do the addition for each problem set. (The numbers of the problems (b) below correspond with those of the problems (a) above. Your teacher may provide you with the answer key so you can check your answers.

4b. _____

5b. _____

6b. _____

7b. _____

8b. _____

9b. _____

10b. _____

Name: _____ Date: _____

Section ③ Finding a Common Denominator

EXTRA PRACTICE   Find the first ten multiples for each number.

1.   5   _____

2.   9   _____

3.   11   _____

4.   6   _____

5.   15   _____

Now find the Least Common Multiple for each pair of numbers.

6.   6, 12 _____   **7.**   4, 8 _____

8.   2, 6 _____   **9.**   3, 9 _____

10. 15, 11 _____   **11.** 6, 5 _____

12. 11, 4 _____   **13.** 7, 9 _____

14. 6, 15 _____   **15.** 10, 9 _____

For each pair of fractions, find the Least Common Denominator.

16. $\frac{2}{9}, \frac{1}{3}$ _____

17. $\frac{4}{11}, \frac{3}{5}$ _____

18. $\frac{7}{12}, \frac{2}{4}$ _____

19. $\frac{3}{15}, \frac{7}{10}$ _____

20. $\frac{1}{6}, \frac{4}{5}$ _____

Name: _____ Date: _____

Section **3** Finding a Common Denominator

EXTRA PRACTICE   For each pair of fractions, convert both to equivalent fractions with a Least Common Denominator so that the pair could be added or subtracted.

1a. $\frac{5}{8}, \frac{13}{15}$ _____ _____

2a. $\frac{3}{4}, \frac{7}{20}$ _____ _____

3a. $\frac{2}{5}, \frac{1}{13}$ _____ _____

4a. $\frac{2}{3}, \frac{3}{4}$ _____ _____

5a. $\frac{3}{9}, \frac{1}{4}$ _____ _____

6a. $\frac{1}{7}, \frac{3}{5}$ _____ _____

7a. $\frac{2}{12}, \frac{5}{7}$ _____ _____

8a. $\frac{5}{10}, \frac{1}{40}$ _____ _____

9a. $\frac{1}{3}, \frac{1}{15}$ _____ _____

10a. $\frac{2}{3}, \frac{5}{8}$ _____ _____

Since you now have the fractions changed into common denominators, go ahead and do the addition for each problem set. The numbers of the problems (b) below correspond with those of the problems (a) above. Your teacher may provide you with the answer key to check your answers.

1b. _____

2b. _____

3b. _____

4b. _____

5b. _____

6b. _____

7b. _____

8b. _____

9b. _____

10b. _____

Name: _____ Date: _____

Section **4** Adding Fractions

ABSORB   Fractions that have a common denominator may be added as shown in the example below.

Example 1: $\frac{3}{10} + \frac{1}{10} =$ _____

$$\frac{3}{10} + \frac{1}{10} = \frac{4}{10}$$

For fractions that do not have a common denominator, a common denominator will need to be found before adding.

Example 2: $\frac{3}{5} + \frac{1}{3} =$ _____

$$\frac{9}{15} + \frac{5}{15} =$$ _____

$$\frac{9}{15} + \frac{5}{15} = \frac{14}{15}$$

APPLY   Add the fractions below. In some of the problems, you will first need to find a common denominator.

1. $\frac{1}{3} + \frac{1}{3} =$ _____

2. $\frac{2}{7} + \frac{3}{7} =$ _____

3. $\frac{5}{6} + \frac{1}{4} =$ _____

4. $\frac{1}{4} + \frac{2}{8} =$ _____

5. $\frac{2}{3} + \frac{1}{4} =$ _____

6. $\frac{3}{6} + \frac{3}{24} =$ _____

7. $\frac{4}{5} + \frac{5}{9} =$ _____

8. $\frac{3}{12} + \frac{5}{36} =$ _____

9. $\frac{7}{8} + \frac{1}{3} =$ _____

10. $\frac{1}{9} + \frac{12}{9} =$ _____

11. $\frac{1}{6} + \frac{2}{6} + \frac{3}{6} =$ _____

12. $\frac{2}{5} + \frac{1}{4} + \frac{3}{5} =$ _____

13. $\frac{5}{8} + \frac{1}{3} + \frac{1}{4} =$ _____

14. $\frac{1}{20} + \frac{3}{20} + \frac{4}{10} =$ _____

15. $\frac{1}{4} + \frac{2}{6} + \frac{3}{12} =$ _____

16. $\frac{4}{5} + \frac{2}{10} + \frac{1}{15} =$ _____

Name: _____ Date: _____

Section 4 Adding Fractions

EXTRA PRACTICE Add the fractions below. In some of the problems, you will first need to find a common denominator.

1. $\frac{1}{4} + \frac{1}{4} =$ _____

2. $\frac{5}{7} + \frac{1}{7} =$ _____

3. $\frac{3}{5} + \frac{1}{3} =$ _____

4. $\frac{1}{2} + \frac{3}{8} =$ _____

5. $\frac{2}{5} + \frac{1}{3} =$ _____

6. $\frac{3}{7} + \frac{2}{15} =$ _____

7. $\frac{3}{5} + \frac{7}{9} =$ _____

8. $\frac{4}{12} + \frac{4}{32} =$ _____

9. $\frac{5}{8} + \frac{1}{4} =$ _____

10. $\frac{1}{8} + \frac{13}{5} =$ _____

11. $\frac{7}{15} + \frac{2}{6} =$ _____

12. $\frac{8}{3} + \frac{6}{12} =$ _____

13. $\frac{10}{7} + \frac{1}{2} =$ _____

14. $\frac{9}{21} + \frac{2}{3} =$ _____

15. $\frac{1}{7} + \frac{1}{2} + \frac{1}{5} =$ _____

16. $\frac{2}{3} + \frac{1}{4} + \frac{3}{8} =$ _____

17. $\frac{5}{9} + \frac{2}{3} + \frac{1}{4} =$ _____

18. $\frac{1}{10} + \frac{3}{12} + \frac{4}{15} =$ _____

19. $\frac{1}{3} + \frac{2}{5} + \frac{3}{14} =$ _____

20. $\frac{4}{6} + \frac{2}{10} + \frac{2}{4} =$ _____

Name: _____ Date: _____

Section ⑤ Subtracting Fractions

ABSORB   Fractions that have a common denominator may be subtracted as shown in the example below.

Example 1: $\frac{21}{40} - \frac{8}{40} =$ _____

$$\frac{21}{40} - \frac{8}{40} = \frac{13}{40}$$

For fractions that do not have a common denominator, a common denominator will need to be found before subtracting.

Example 2: $\frac{4}{5} - \frac{3}{10} =$ _____

$$\frac{8}{10} - \frac{3}{10} =$$ _____

$$\frac{8}{10} - \frac{3}{10} = \frac{5}{10}$$

APPLY   Subtract the fractions below. In some of the problems, you will first need to find a common denominator.

1. $\frac{2}{5} - \frac{1}{5} =$ _____

2. $\frac{4}{3} - \frac{2}{3} =$ _____

3. $\frac{13}{7} - \frac{10}{7} =$ _____

4. $\frac{6}{13} - \frac{12}{39} =$ _____

5. $\frac{18}{20} - \frac{2}{10} =$ _____

6. $\frac{6}{25} - \frac{1}{10} =$ _____

7. $\frac{3}{8} - \frac{1}{24} =$ _____

8. $\frac{200}{120} - \frac{90}{120} =$ _____

9. $\frac{7}{16} - \frac{1}{8} =$ _____

10. $\frac{20}{40} - \frac{1}{20} =$ _____

11. $\frac{6}{5} - \frac{3}{4} =$ _____

12. $\frac{2}{9} - \frac{1}{81} =$ _____

13. $\frac{2}{11} - \frac{1}{22} =$ _____

14. $\frac{16}{15} - \frac{12}{30} =$ _____

15. $\frac{10}{15} - \frac{1}{5} =$ _____

16. $\frac{1}{1} - \frac{8}{9} =$ _____

Name: _____ Date: _____

Section 5 Subtracting Fractions

EXTRA PRACTICE   Subtract the fractions below. In some of the problems, you will first need to find a common denominator.

1. $\frac{3}{5} - \frac{2}{5} =$ _____

2. $\frac{5}{3} - \frac{1}{3} =$ _____

3. $\frac{13}{5} - \frac{10}{5} =$ _____

4. $\frac{6}{12} - \frac{12}{32} =$ _____

5. $\frac{18}{30} - \frac{2}{20} =$ _____

6. $\frac{6}{15} - \frac{1}{9} =$ _____

7. $\frac{3}{7} - \frac{1}{25} =$ _____

8. $\frac{200}{150} - \frac{90}{100} =$ _____

9. $\frac{7}{15} - \frac{1}{7} =$ _____

10. $\frac{20}{30} - \frac{1}{30} =$ _____

11. $\frac{6}{4} - \frac{3}{5} =$ _____

12. $\frac{2}{8} - \frac{2}{80} =$ _____

13. $\frac{2}{10} - \frac{1}{20} =$ _____

14. $\frac{16}{12} - \frac{12}{20} =$ _____

15. $\frac{10}{12} - \frac{1}{4} =$ _____

16. $\frac{2}{2} - \frac{7}{8} =$ _____

17. $\frac{15}{3} - \frac{4}{4} =$ _____

18. $\frac{89}{76} - \frac{14}{76} =$ _____

19. $\frac{6}{14} - \frac{2}{7} =$ _____

20. $\frac{3}{5} - \frac{1}{4} =$ _____

Name: _____ Date: _____

Section **6** Reducing Fractions

ABSORB   We'll take a breather from adding and subtracting fractions to look at something that will make computations with fractions much easier.

First, we need to review the term **factor**. Look at the factors of 12 listed below.

Factors are: 1, 2, 3, 4, 6, 12   because 1 x 12 = 12, 2 x 6 = 12, 3 x 4 = 12

If the numerator and denominator of a fraction share a common factor, then that fraction can be reduced to a simpler form.

Here's how it works:

$\frac{12}{18}$ can be reduced because 6 is a factor of both numbers.

6 x 2 = 12 and 6 x 3 = 18.

So, $\frac{12}{18}$ can be reduced to $\frac{2}{3}$.

The key to reducing fractions is the ability to spot the **Greatest Common Factor** (GCF) between two numbers (if there is one) and to use it to reduce the fraction as shown above.

If a numerator and denominator have no common factors, then the fraction is already in its reduced form. (It's understood that 1 is a factor of every number, but that will not help to reduce a fraction.)

Before we try reducing any fractions, we'll brush up on finding the factors of numbers.

APPLY   For each number below, list all its factors.

1.   18   _____

2.   21   _____

3.   24   _____

4.   15   _____

Now for each pair of numbers below, find the Greatest Common Factor (GCF).

5.   24, 36   _____

6.   16, 32   _____

7.   10, 50   _____

8.   8, 48   _____

9.   12, 44   _____

10.   18, 27   _____

Name: _____ Date: _____

Section **6** Reducing Fractions

EXTRA PRACTICE   For each number below, list all its factors.

1.   30   _____

2.   72   _____

3.   25   _____

4.   48   _____

5.   81   _____

For each pair of numbers below, find the Greatest Common Factor (GCF).

6.   12, 48   _____   **7.**   15, 30   _____

8.   20, 40   _____   **9.**   9, 56   _____

10.   11, 33   _____   **11.**   14, 28   _____

12.   36, 81   _____   **13.**   14, 21   _____

14.   30, 45   _____   **15.**   24, 60   _____

Now find the Greatest Common Factor for the numerator and denominator in each fraction below.

16. $\frac{3}{21}$ _____

17. $\frac{8}{16}$ _____

18. $\frac{20}{24}$ _____

19. $\frac{15}{35}$ _____

20. $\frac{22}{77}$ _____

Name: _____ Date: _____

Section 7 More About Reducing Fractions

ABSORB   Now let's take a look at a couple of reduced fractions, written in factored form to reveal the **Greatest Common Factor** (GCF).

Original Fraction	GCF	Factored Process	Reduced Form
$\frac{4}{12}$	4	$\frac{1 \times 4}{3 \times 4}$	$\frac{1}{3}$
$\frac{21}{24}$	3	$\frac{7 \times 3}{8 \times 3}$	$\frac{7}{8}$

To reduce a fraction, you find the GCF and then divide the numerator and denominator by that number.

Original Fraction	GCF	Divide	Reduced Form
$\frac{4}{12}$	4	$\frac{4 \div 4}{12 \div 4}$	$\frac{1}{3}$
$\frac{21}{24}$	3	$\frac{21 \div 3}{24 \div 3}$	$\frac{7}{8}$

APPLY   Reduce each of the fractions given to lowest terms. Write "reduced" if the fraction is already in its simplest form.

1. $\frac{6}{10}$ _____

2. $\frac{2}{39}$ _____

3. $\frac{8}{16}$ _____

4. $\frac{5}{15}$ _____

5. $\frac{4}{48}$ _____

6. $\frac{7}{28}$ _____

7. $\frac{3}{15}$ _____

8. $\frac{3}{9}$ _____

9. $\frac{2}{27}$ _____

10. $\frac{8}{18}$ _____

Name: _____ Date: _____

Section **7** More About Reducing Fractions

EXTRA PRACTICE Reduce each of the fractions given to lowest terms. Write "reduced" if the fraction is already in its simplest form.

1. $\frac{3}{23}$ _____

2. $\frac{2}{50}$ _____

3. $\frac{9}{45}$ _____

4. $\frac{3}{17}$ _____

5. $\frac{12}{60}$ _____

6. $\frac{11}{41}$ _____

7. $\frac{10}{110}$ _____

8. $\frac{120}{200}$ _____

9. $\frac{15}{18}$ _____

10. $\frac{16}{64}$ _____

11. $\frac{6}{12}$ _____

12. $\frac{2}{40}$ _____

13. $\frac{8}{24}$ _____

14. $\frac{5}{25}$ _____

15. $\frac{4}{44}$ _____

16. $\frac{7}{21}$ _____

17. $\frac{3}{10}$ _____

18. $\frac{3}{27}$ _____

19. $\frac{2}{25}$ _____

20. $\frac{22}{33}$ _____

21. $\frac{3}{25}$ _____

22. $\frac{28}{49}$ _____

23. $\frac{9}{56}$ _____

24. $\frac{3}{18}$ _____

25. $\frac{12}{50}$ _____

26. $\frac{11}{32}$ _____

27. $\frac{10}{120}$ _____

28. $\frac{120}{250}$ _____

29. $\frac{15}{19}$ _____

30. $\frac{18}{81}$ _____

Name: _____ Date: _____

Section 8 Improper Fractions

ABSORB

Did you notice in Sections 4 and 5 on adding and subtracting fractions that some of the answers had a larger numerator than denominator? This is called an **improper fraction**.

When the numerator is larger than the denominator, it simply means that the fraction can actually be converted into a whole number or a whole number with a fractions portion.

Look at the following illustration:

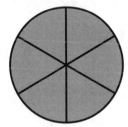 

The shaded portions of these circles can be described by the fraction $\frac{7}{6}$. Do you see why $\frac{6}{6}$ represents one whole circle in this example? $\frac{1}{6}$ would therefore represent the shaded portion of the second circle. So this quantity would actually be written as $1\frac{1}{6}$ once the improper fraction was properly reduced.

Each time the numerator is equivalent to the denominator, a whole number has been "accumulated" by the fraction. The fraction $\frac{8}{4}$ would actually reduce to 2 wholes, or simply 2. Likewise, $\frac{9}{4}$ would reduce to $2\frac{1}{4}$.

APPLY

Reduce each improper fraction to a whole number or a whole number with a fractional part. Drawing the fractions as was done in the illustration above may be useful.

1. $\frac{5}{3}$ _____

2. $\frac{7}{2}$ _____

3. $\frac{8}{5}$ _____

4. $\frac{10}{2}$ _____

5. $\frac{12}{5}$ _____

6. $\frac{21}{8}$ _____

7. $\frac{20}{10}$ _____

8. $\frac{4}{3}$ _____

9. $\frac{6}{1}$ _____

10. $\frac{13}{6}$ _____

Name:_____ Date:_____

Section **8** Improper Fractions

EXTRA PRACTICE Reduce each improper fraction to a whole number or a whole number with a fractional part. Reduce the fractional part to simplest form if needed. Drawing a picture to illustrate the fraction may be useful.

1. $\frac{5}{4}$ _____

2. $\frac{7}{3}$ _____

3. $\frac{8}{4}$ _____

4. $\frac{10}{3}$ _____

5. $\frac{12}{6}$ _____

6. $\frac{21}{9}$ _____

7. $\frac{20}{15}$ _____

8. $\frac{4}{2}$ _____

9. $\frac{6}{2}$ _____

10. $\frac{13}{1}$ _____

11. $\frac{9}{2}$ _____

12. $\frac{18}{4}$ _____

13. $\frac{15}{12}$ _____

14. $\frac{42}{32}$ _____

15. $\frac{72}{8}$ _____

16. $\frac{50}{6}$ _____

17. $\frac{29}{25}$ _____

18. $\frac{31}{7}$ _____

19. $\frac{110}{10}$ _____

20. $\frac{19}{3}$ _____

Name: _____ Date: _____

Section Review ① Covering Sections 1 Through 8

APPLY Complete the exercises below. In answering questions, fractions should be written in their reduced form.

Write a fraction to describe each situation.

1. Six dogs ran across the street, but one turned around and went back. Express the portion that continued across the street.

_____

2. Forty-one of 80 people did not like the new design for the latest smart phone. Express the portion who did not like the new design.

_____

3. Ten cars out of 200 cars crossing the intersection were seen to have an expired inspection sticker. Express the portion that did not have an expired inspection sticker.

_____

Find the first 8 multiples for each number.

4. 4 _____

5. 13 _____

Find the Least Common Multiple (LCM) for each number pair.

6. 4, 24 _____

7. 8, 20 _____

8. 30, 50 _____

For each pair of fractions, name the Least Common Denominator (LCD).

9. $\frac{6}{8}, \frac{2}{12}$ _____   **10.** $\frac{1}{20}, \frac{3}{15}$ _____   **11.** $\frac{7}{8}, \frac{9}{64}$ _____

Name: _____ Date: _____

Section Review ① Covering Sections 1 Through 8

For each of the numbers below, list all its factors.

12. 36 _____

13. 51 _____

14. 100 _____

15. 27 _____

For each pair of numbers, find the Greatest Common Factor (GCF).

16. 12, 120 _____

17. 16, 64 _____

18. 3, 90 _____

19. 4, 52 _____

20. 4, 16 _____

21. 6, 7 _____

22. 5, 7 _____

23. 3, 11 _____

Add or subtract as indicated in each problem. Reduce each answer to lowest terms.

24. $\frac{1}{8} + \frac{5}{8} =$ _____

25. $\frac{4}{14} + \frac{1}{56} =$ _____

26. $\frac{2}{7} + \frac{4}{5} =$ _____

27. $\frac{9}{8} - \frac{5}{8} =$ _____

28. $\frac{6}{9} - \frac{2}{12} =$ _____

29. $\frac{20}{12} - \frac{1}{1} =$ _____

30. $\frac{12}{14} - \frac{1}{14} =$ _____

31. $\frac{25}{4} - \frac{7}{8} =$ _____

32. $\frac{105}{15} - \frac{25}{40} =$ _____

33. $\frac{160}{90} - \frac{70}{180} =$ _____

34. $\frac{1}{6} + \frac{1}{4} + \frac{1}{3} =$ _____

35. $\frac{2}{3} + \frac{5}{8} + \frac{1}{12} + \frac{2}{24} =$ _____

Name: _____   Date: _____

Section Review (1) Covering Sections 1 Through 8

EXTRA PRACTICE Complete the exercises below. In answering questions, fractions should be written in their reduced form.

Write a fraction to describe each situation.

1. Eight students were given a chance to retake the math test. Seven students did better the second time. Express the portion of students who did not do better on the second test.

_____

2. Twenty-nine of 55 people surveyed said they would buy an electric car if it was affordable. Express the portion who said they would buy an electric car.

_____

Find the first 8 multiples of the following number.

3. 5   _____

Find the Least Common Multiple for each number pair.

4. 5, 25 _____   **5.** 9, 30 _____

For each pair of fractions, name the Least Common Denominator.

6. $\frac{6}{9}$, $\frac{2}{15}$ _____   **7.** $\frac{1}{30}$, $\frac{3}{25}$ _____

For each of the numbers below, list all its factors.

8. 35 _____   **9.** 52 _____

For each pair of numbers, find the Greatest Common Factor.

10. 13, 130 _____   **11.** 4, 80 _____

Add or subtract as indicated in each problem. Reduce each answer to lowest terms.

12. $\frac{1}{9} + \frac{5}{9} =$ _____   **13.** $\frac{2}{8} + \frac{4}{6} =$ _____

14. $\frac{9}{7} - \frac{5}{7} =$ _____   **15.** $\frac{20}{15} - \frac{2}{2} =$ _____

Name: _____ Date: _____

Section 9 Converting Fractions to Decimal Numbers

ABSORB A fraction is essentially a division problem. Consider the improper fraction $\frac{10}{2}$. If we write this fraction as its equivalent division problem, it will look something like this:

10 ÷ 2 = _____

We know that $\frac{10}{2}$ can be reduced to the whole number 5. Likewise, we know the answer to 10 ÷ 2 is also 5.

All fractions can be converted to decimal numbers. Consider the fraction $\frac{4}{5}$. If we write this as a division problem, it will look something like this:

4 ÷ 5 = _____

The answer, once the division is done, will be 0.80. This makes sense in terms of a reasonable answer, because we know $\frac{4}{5}$ must be less than 1, and 0.80 is also less than 1.

Since working with fractions is the purpose of this book (more so than relearning long division), it is suggested that you use a calculator to help with the exercises below.

APPLY Convert the fractions given to decimal numbers. Many fractions produce repeating decimals, but we'll limit our answers to writing the first four digits past the decimal and rounding when applicable, i.e., 1.6667.

1. $\frac{1}{2}$ _____   2. $\frac{4}{10}$ _____

3. $\frac{1}{3}$ _____   4. $\frac{3}{8}$ _____

5. $\frac{1}{4}$ _____   6. $\frac{5}{9}$ _____

7. $\frac{1}{5}$ _____   8. $\frac{6}{7}$ _____

9. $\frac{1}{6}$ _____   10. $\frac{2}{11}$ _____

11. $\frac{1}{7}$ _____   12. $\frac{4}{25}$ _____

13. $\frac{1}{8}$ _____   14. $\frac{11}{50}$ _____

15. $\frac{1}{9}$ _____   16. $\frac{13}{19}$ _____

Section 9 Converting Fractions to Decimal Numbers

EXTRA PRACTICE Convert the fractions given to decimal numbers. Many fractions produce repeating decimals, but we'll limit our answers to writing the first four digits past the decimal point and rounding when applicable, i.e., 1.6667. You may use a calculator.

1. $\frac{2}{3}$ _____

2. $\frac{8}{10}$ _____

3. $\frac{7}{14}$ _____

4. $\frac{3}{9}$ _____

5. $\frac{9}{24}$ _____

6. $\frac{5}{8}$ _____

7. $\frac{8}{32}$ _____

8. $\frac{6}{8}$ _____

9. $\frac{1}{20}$ _____

10. $\frac{2}{12}$ _____

11. $\frac{35}{50}$ _____

12. $\frac{4}{20}$ _____

13. $\frac{4}{26}$ _____

14. $\frac{11}{45}$ _____

15. $\frac{70}{100}$ _____

16. $\frac{13}{15}$ _____

17. $\frac{1}{30}$ _____

18. $\frac{2}{42}$ _____

19. $\frac{43}{79}$ _____

20. $\frac{9}{54}$ _____

Convert the following improper fractions to decimals. These fractions will produce decimals that are greater than 1. If the decimal repeats, limit your answer to four digits past the decimal point and round when applicable.

21. $\frac{8}{3}$ _____

22. $\frac{14}{5}$ _____

23. $\frac{4}{2}$ _____

24. $\frac{17}{6}$ _____

25. $\frac{42}{8}$ _____

26. $\frac{90}{5}$ _____

27. $\frac{64}{3}$ _____

28. $\frac{27}{4}$ _____

29. $\frac{115}{16}$ _____

30. $\frac{250}{75}$ _____

Name: _____ Date: _____

Section **10** Ordering Fractions

ABSORB   In previous sections, we have learned how to reduce fractions and also how to convert fractions to decimal numbers.

The **numerator ÷ denominator** gives us a quick way to convert a fraction to a decimal number. It also provides a quick way to compare fractions based on their size. By changing two fractions to decimal numbers, you can tell which number is larger.

Example: Compare $\frac{3}{4}$ and $\frac{4}{9}$.

$$\frac{3}{4} = 0.75 \quad \text{and} \quad \frac{4}{9} = 0.4444$$

$\frac{3}{4}$ is greater than $\frac{4}{9}$.

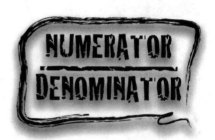

APPLY   For the following fraction pairs, use the symbols < "less than," > "greater than," and = "equal to" to correctly complete the expression. Change the fractions to decimal numbers so you can easily compare the numbers.

1. $\frac{5}{6}$ _____ $\frac{4}{5}$

2. $\frac{4}{13}$ _____ $\frac{2}{7}$

3. $\frac{5}{2}$ _____ $\frac{4}{3}$

4. $\frac{3}{12}$ _____ $\frac{1}{4}$

5. $\frac{2}{3}$ _____ $\frac{3}{5}$

6. $\frac{40}{5}$ _____ $\frac{120}{20}$

7. $\frac{13}{10}$ _____ $\frac{15}{10}$

8. 1.65 _____ $1\frac{2}{5}$

9. $\frac{7}{8}$ _____ $\frac{17}{20}$

10. 0.75 _____ $\frac{4}{5}$

In this section, three numbers are written for each problem, including fractions, decimals, and whole numbers. Rewrite the numbers on the line in order from least to greatest. If they are already in correct order, write "correct."

11. $\frac{1}{2}, \frac{6}{8}, 0.60$ _____

12. $\frac{12}{5}, \frac{8}{3}, \frac{9}{7}$ _____

13. $3.12, 3\frac{3}{12}, 2.99$ _____

14. $7.1, \frac{7}{6}, \frac{4}{3}$ _____

15. $\frac{6}{5}, \frac{5}{3}, \frac{9}{5}$ _____

16. $100, 1.100, 0.100$ _____

17. $11, \frac{111}{11}, 10\frac{1}{2}$ _____

18. $\frac{11}{44}, \frac{1}{5}, \frac{3}{8}$ _____

Name: _____   Date: _____

Section 10 Ordering Fractions

EXTRA PRACTICE   For the following fraction pairs, use the symbols < "less than," > "greater than," and = "equal to" to correctly complete the expression. Change the fractions to decimal numbers so you can easily compare the numbers.

1. $\frac{5}{8}$ _____ $\frac{4}{5}$ 2. $\frac{4}{12}$ _____ $\frac{2}{5}$

3. $\frac{5}{3}$ _____ $\frac{4}{2}$ 4. $\frac{3}{15}$ _____ $\frac{1}{3}$

5. $\frac{2}{3}$ _____ $\frac{3}{4}$ 6. $\frac{40}{6}$ _____ $\frac{120}{30}$

7. $\frac{13}{9}$ _____ $\frac{15}{8}$ 8. 1.55 _____ $1\frac{2}{3}$

9. $\frac{7}{9}$ _____ $\frac{17}{25}$ 10. 0.25 _____ $\frac{4}{3}$

In this section, three numbers are written for each problem, including fractions, decimals, and whole numbers. Rewrite the numbers on the line in order from least to greatest. If they are already in correct order, write "correct."

11. $\frac{1}{3}$, $\frac{6}{8}$, 0.5 _____   12. $\frac{12}{8}$, $\frac{8}{5}$, $\frac{9}{6}$ _____

13. 3.25, $3\frac{3}{15}$, 2.88 _____   14. 7.2, $\frac{7}{5}$, $\frac{4}{2}$ _____

15. $\frac{6}{4}$, $\frac{5}{2}$, $\frac{9}{4}$ _____   16. 200, 2.200, 0.22 _____

17. 12, $\frac{122}{22}$, $12\frac{2}{3}$ _____   18. $\frac{11}{22}$, $\frac{1}{4}$, $\frac{3}{9}$ _____

19. $\frac{7}{8}$, 0.85, $1\frac{2}{3}$ _____   20. 5.1, $5\frac{3}{10}$, $\frac{50}{10}$ _____

Section 11 Adding Mixed Numbers and Improper Fractions

ABSORB   We learned in previous sections that finding a common denominator was a first step in adding basic fractions. But what if the fractions have whole number portions or are improper fractions? Here's a checklist for adding **mixed numbers** (whole numbers with fractional parts) and **improper fractions** (fractions where the numerator is larger than the denominator).

▸ If an improper fraction is involved, reduce it to a whole number or a whole number with a fractional part.

▸ If there are any whole numbers involved, ignore them for a moment and concentrate on getting a common denominator for the fractions involved.

▸ Add the fractions after getting a common denominator for them.

▸ Now go back and add up all the whole numbers and express your answer. Is your answer an improper fraction or a fraction that needs to be reduced? Take care of that in this step.

Example 1:

$$2\frac{6}{8} + \frac{7}{6} =$$

$$2\frac{6}{8} + 1\frac{1}{6} =$$

$$2\frac{18}{24} + 1\frac{4}{24} =$$

$$2\frac{18}{24} + 1\frac{4}{24} = 3\frac{22}{24}$$

reduces to: $3\frac{11}{12}$

Example 2:

$$\frac{88}{18} + 1\frac{8}{3} =$$

$$4\frac{16}{18} + (1 + 2\frac{2}{3}) =$$

$$4\frac{16}{18} + 3\frac{12}{18} =$$

$$4\frac{16}{18} + 3\frac{12}{18} = 7\frac{28}{18}$$

reduces to: $8\frac{5}{9}$

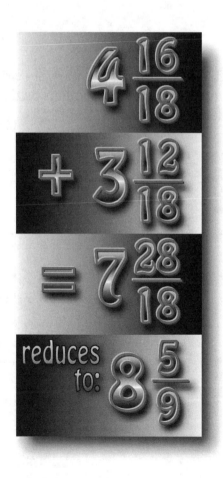

$$4\frac{16}{18}$$

$$+3\frac{12}{18}$$

$$=7\frac{28}{18}$$

reduces to: $8\frac{5}{9}$

Name: _____ Date: _____

APPLY Solve the problems below by adding the fractions. Reduce each answer to lowest terms.

1. $\frac{4}{5} + \frac{9}{5} =$ _____

2. $\frac{3}{4} + \frac{14}{3} =$ _____

3. $\frac{21}{12} + \frac{16}{4} =$ _____

4. $\frac{34}{6} + 1\frac{1}{2} =$ _____

5. $\frac{69}{60} + \frac{21}{4} =$ _____

6. $\frac{120}{3} + 2\frac{10}{24} =$ _____

7. $30\frac{3}{8} + 12\frac{5}{8} =$ _____

8. $\frac{22}{10} + \frac{21}{10} =$ _____

9. $2\frac{1}{7} + 1\frac{9}{7} =$ _____

10. $3\frac{4}{40} + 2\frac{11}{4} =$ _____

11. $\frac{124}{12} + \frac{18}{3} =$ _____

12. $\frac{28}{56} + \frac{1}{2} =$ _____

13. $\frac{9}{72} + \frac{72}{9} =$ _____

14. $2\frac{1}{44} + \frac{39}{11} =$ _____

15. $\frac{53}{11} + 1\frac{5}{8} =$ _____

Name: _____ Date: _____

<table>
<tr><td>Section</td><td>11</td><td colspan="2"># Adding Mixed Numbers and Improper Fractions</td></tr>
</table>

EXTRA PRACTICE   Solve the problems below by adding the fractions. Reduce each answer to lowest terms.

1. $\frac{4}{6} + \frac{9}{4} =$ _____

2. $\frac{3}{5} + \frac{14}{4} =$ _____

3. $\frac{21}{15} + \frac{16}{3} =$ _____

4. $\frac{34}{5} + 1\frac{1}{3} =$ _____

5. $\frac{69}{62} + \frac{21}{3} =$ _____

6. $\frac{120}{4} + 2\frac{10}{25} =$ _____

7. $30\frac{3}{5} + 12\frac{5}{9} =$ _____

8. $\frac{22}{15} + \frac{21}{15} =$ _____

9. $2\frac{1}{8} + 1\frac{9}{8} =$ _____

10. $3\frac{4}{40} + 2\frac{11}{5} =$ _____

11. $\frac{125}{15} + \frac{18}{9} =$ _____

12. $\frac{28}{55} + \frac{1}{4} =$ _____

13. $\frac{9}{75} + \frac{75}{9} =$ _____

14. $2\frac{1}{45} + \frac{39}{12} =$ _____

15. $\frac{53}{12} + 1\frac{5}{9} =$ _____

Section 12 Subtracting Mixed Numbers and Improper Fractions

ABSORB

We learned in previous sections that finding a common denominator was a first step in subtracting fractions. But what if the fractions have whole number portions or are improper fractions? What if borrowing needs to take place before the subtraction can be accomplished? Here's a checklist for subtracting **mixed numbers** (whole numbers with fractional parts) and **improper fractions** (fractions where the numerator is larger than the denominator).

▸ If an improper fraction is being subtracted, reduce it to a whole number or a whole number with a fractional part.

▸ Find a common denominator for the fractional portions involved.

▸ Is borrowing required? If so, make the conversion.

▸ Perform the subtraction required. Does the final answer need to be reduced? If so, take care of that in this step.

Example 1:

$$2\frac{2}{8} - \frac{4}{5} =$$

$$2\frac{10}{40} - \frac{32}{40} =$$

$$1 + \left(\frac{40}{40} + \frac{10}{40}\right) - \frac{32}{40} =$$

$$2\frac{50}{40} - \frac{32}{40} =$$

$$2\frac{50}{40} - \frac{32}{40} = 1\frac{18}{40}$$

reduces to: $1\frac{9}{20}$

Example 2:

$$4\frac{2}{3} - \frac{7}{2} =$$

$$4\frac{2}{3} - 3\frac{1}{2} =$$

$$4\frac{4}{6} - 3\frac{3}{6} =$$

$$4\frac{4}{6} - 3\frac{3}{6} = 1\frac{1}{6}$$

Name: _____ Date: _____

Section **12** Subtracting Mixed Numbers and Improper Fractions

APPLY Solve the problems below by subtracting the fractions. Reduce each answer to lowest terms.

1. $\frac{3}{4} - \frac{1}{8} =$ _____

2. $1\frac{4}{9} - \frac{6}{9} =$ _____

3. $12\frac{1}{7} - 3\frac{5}{6} =$ _____

4. $4 - 2\frac{2}{3} =$ _____

5. $30\frac{1}{12} - 12\frac{7}{10} =$ _____

6. $20\frac{5}{8} - 5\frac{1}{4} =$ _____

7. $3\frac{7}{8} - 1 =$ _____

8. $7\frac{7}{8} - 6\frac{5}{9} =$ _____

9. $3\frac{3}{32} - 1\frac{9}{16} =$ _____

10. $5\frac{5}{8} - 2\frac{1}{4} =$ _____

11. $\frac{20}{4} - \frac{9}{12} =$ _____

12. $13\frac{12}{24} - \frac{114}{10} =$ _____

13. $90 - \frac{90}{10} =$ _____

14. $16\frac{4}{3} - \frac{9}{4} =$ _____

15. $\frac{23}{10} - \frac{4}{6} =$ _____

Name: _____ Date: _____

Section **12** Subtracting Mixed Numbers and Improper Fractions

EXTRA PRACTICE   Solve the problems below by subtracting the fractions. Reduce each answer to lowest terms.

1. $\frac{3}{5} - \frac{1}{9} =$ _____

2. $1\frac{4}{8} - \frac{6}{8} =$ _____

3. $12\frac{1}{6} - 3\frac{5}{8} =$ _____

4. $4 - 2\frac{2}{5} =$ _____

5. $30\frac{1}{15} - 12\frac{7}{15} =$ _____

6. $20\frac{5}{9} - 5\frac{1}{3} =$ _____

7. $3\frac{7}{9} - 2 =$ _____

8. $7\frac{7}{9} - 6\frac{5}{8} =$ _____

9. $3\frac{3}{35} - 1\frac{9}{17} =$ _____

10. $5\frac{5}{9} - 2\frac{1}{5} =$ _____

11. $\frac{20}{5} - \frac{9}{15} =$ _____

12. $13\frac{12}{25} - \frac{115}{20} =$ _____

13. $70 - \frac{70}{20} =$ _____

14. $16\frac{3}{2} - \frac{9}{5} =$ _____

15. $\frac{23}{15} - \frac{4}{5} =$ _____

Name: _____   Date: _____

Section	13	More Practice Adding and Subtracting Fractions

APPLY

Add or subtract as indicated. In most of the problems, it will be necessary to find a common denominator. Make sure that fractions have been fully reduced in your answers.

1. $\frac{12}{16} + 3\frac{9}{16} =$ _____

2. $\frac{23}{8} + \frac{5}{7} =$ _____

3. $\frac{1}{2} - \frac{2}{8} =$ _____

4. $\frac{4}{5} - \frac{2}{12} =$ _____

5. $2\frac{24}{48} + \frac{30}{36} =$ _____

6. $4 - \frac{7}{8} =$ _____

7. $3\frac{1}{2} - \frac{8}{3} =$ _____

8. $\frac{20}{6} - \frac{13}{5} =$ _____

9. $12 + 1\frac{9}{12} =$ _____

10. $16\frac{1}{8} - 2\frac{6}{9} =$ _____

11. $\frac{5}{22} + \frac{3}{10} =$ _____

12. $\frac{80}{3} - 12\frac{5}{7} =$ _____

13. $\frac{100}{9} + 2\frac{7}{27} + \frac{4}{18} =$ _____

14. $\frac{21}{4} + 1\frac{5}{16} + 2\frac{3}{8} =$ _____

15. $11\frac{20}{40} - 1\frac{78}{80} =$ _____

16. $5\frac{1}{8} - 2\frac{56}{72} =$ _____

Name: _____   Date: _____

More Practice Adding and Subtracting Fractions

APPLY   Solve the following word problems involving addition or subtraction of fractions.

17. Three barrels of the same size are each partially full of grain. One is $\frac{2}{3}$ full. Another is $\frac{1}{2}$ full. The remaining one is $\frac{3}{8}$ full. How much total grain is there?

_____

18. A large water tank is $\frac{2}{9}$ full. What fraction could be used to describe the empty portion of the tank?

_____

19. A piece of cardboard had $\frac{2}{5}$ of its usable area cut off. How much of the original piece of cardboard remains?

_____

20. Alan opened four 1-gallon containers of orange juice for a party. After the party, one container was empty. One container had about $\frac{1}{2}$ the original amount of juice remaining. Each of the other two containers looked to be about $\frac{1}{3}$ full. Approximately how much juice was left over from the party?

_____

_____

21. A large sheet cake was cut into 24 pieces. Seventeen of the pieces were served to guests. What portion of the sheet cake was not served?

_____

22. Corey split a large piece of clay into seven equal parts. He used three of those pieces to make a sculpture, which he gave as a gift to a friend. What portion of the clay is still available for another project?

_____

Name: _____   Date: _____

Section **13** More Practice Adding and Subtracting Fractions

EXTRA PRACTICE   Add or subtract as indicated. In most of the problems, it will be necessary to find a common denominator. Make sure that fractions have been fully reduced in your answers.

1. $2\frac{24}{50} + \frac{30}{35} =$ _____

2. $3\frac{1}{4} - \frac{8}{5} =$ _____

3. $\frac{5}{20} + \frac{3}{9} =$ _____

4. $\frac{80}{4} - 12\frac{5}{8} =$ _____

5. $\frac{23}{9} + \frac{5}{6} =$ _____

6. $\frac{1}{3} - \frac{2}{9} =$ _____

Solve the following word problems involving addition or subtraction of fractions.

7.   A large barrel is $\frac{2}{8}$ full of oil. What is the fraction of the empty portion?

_____

8.   A pizza was cut into 9 pieces and 6 pieces were served to guests. What portion remains?

_____

9.   There are three bottles of glue in the classroom. One is $\frac{3}{4}$ full. The second is about $\frac{2}{3}$ full. The third bottle is $\frac{1}{4}$ full. How many total bottles of glue are there?

_____

10.   Marcy used up $\frac{5}{6}$ of a skein of yarn on the doll blanket she knitted. How much yarn remains?

_____

11.   Kyle has three boxes of nails left over from various carpentry projects. One box is $\frac{1}{5}$ full. Another is $\frac{1}{8}$ full, and the last one is $\frac{1}{2}$ full. How many total boxes of nails does he have?

_____

12.   Sherrie was making dinner rolls. She divided her dough into 20 pieces. She used 11 pieces to make rolls for her Thanksgiving dinner. What portion of the dough did she freeze to use later?

_____

Name: _____ Date: _____

Section Review 2 Covering Sections 1 Through 13

APPLY For each pair of fractions, name the Least Common Denominator that could be used for the pair.

1. $\frac{1}{4}, \frac{5}{6}$ _____

2. $\frac{3}{16}, \frac{5}{12}$ _____

3. $\frac{3}{8}, \frac{1}{64}$ _____

List all factors for the following numbers.

4. 22 _____

5. 48 _____

6. 32 _____

7. 45 _____

For each pair of numbers, find the Greatest Common Factor.

8. 6, 16 _____

9. 4, 14 _____

10. 12, 60 _____

11. 3, 16 _____

12. 20, 100 _____

13. 7, 21 _____

Reduce the fractions to lowest terms. For improper fractions, write a whole number or a whole number with a fractional portion in lowest terms.

14. $\frac{6}{9}$ _____

15. $\frac{40}{50}$ _____

16. $\frac{3}{12}$ _____

17. $\frac{10}{6}$ _____

18. $\frac{10}{3}$ _____

19. $\frac{14}{32}$ _____

Convert the fractions to decimal equivalents. Limit your answer to four places past the decimal point.

20. $\frac{3}{16}$ _____

21. $\frac{1}{15}$ _____

22. $\frac{3}{8}$ _____

23. $\frac{6}{8}$ _____

24. $\frac{4}{7}$ _____

25. $\frac{1}{8}$ _____

26. $\frac{5}{3}$ _____

27. $\frac{5}{9}$ _____

28. $\frac{8}{2}$ _____

29. $\frac{7}{10}$ _____

Name: _____ Date: _____

Section Review ❷ Covering Sections 1 Through 13

For the following fraction pairs, use <, >, or = to correctly complete the expression.

30. $\frac{1}{2}$ _____ $\frac{5}{8}$

31. $\frac{12}{5}$ _____ $\frac{13}{6}$

32. $\frac{6}{7}$ _____ $\frac{7}{9}$

33. $\frac{2}{3}$ _____ $\frac{3}{5}$

34. $\frac{13}{15}$ _____ $\frac{12}{14}$

35. $\frac{1}{9}$ _____ $\frac{3}{15}$

Add or subtract as indicated. All answers should be in reduced form.

36. $\frac{14}{3} - \frac{2}{3} =$ _____

37. $\frac{4}{9} - \frac{3}{18} =$ _____

38. $1\frac{1}{2} - \frac{7}{8} =$ _____

39. $2\frac{1}{10} + \frac{11}{10} =$ _____

40. $3 + \frac{1}{3} =$ _____

41. $5\frac{1}{4} - \frac{8}{9} =$ _____

42. $2\frac{3}{16} + 1\frac{12}{32} =$ _____

43. $\frac{17}{20} + \frac{13}{20} =$ _____

44. $10\frac{1}{8} - 2\frac{5}{7} =$ _____

45. $3 - \frac{12}{28} =$ _____

46. $\frac{1}{5} + \frac{1}{6} + \frac{1}{4} =$ _____

47. $\frac{2}{12} + \frac{3}{8} + \frac{1}{36} =$ _____

48. $24 - \frac{24}{3} =$ _____

Name: _____   Date: _____

Section Review 2 Covering Sections 1 Through 13

EXTRA PRACTICE For each pair of fractions, name the Least Common Denominator that could be used for the pair.

1. $\frac{1}{3}, \frac{5}{7}$ _____

2. $\frac{3}{15}, \frac{5}{10}$ _____

3. $\frac{4}{7}, \frac{11}{5}$ _____

List all factors for the following numbers.

4. 20 _____

5. 68 _____

6. 96 _____

7. 36 _____

For each pair of numbers, find the Greatest Common Factor.

8. 5, 15 _____

9. 7, 17 _____

10. 15, 45 _____

11. 8, 42 _____

12. 24, 60 _____

13. 25, 70 _____

Reduce the fractions to lowest terms. For improper fractions, write a whole number or a whole number with a fractional portion in lowest terms.

14. $\frac{6}{8}$ _____

15. $\frac{40}{60}$ _____

16. $\frac{3}{15}$ _____

17. $\frac{18}{3}$ _____

18. $\frac{36}{54}$ _____

19. $\frac{29}{5}$ _____

Convert the fractions to decimal equivalents. Limit your answer to four places past the decimal point.

20. $\frac{3}{12}$ _____

21. $\frac{1}{20}$ _____

22. $\frac{3}{9}$ _____

23. $\frac{6}{9}$ _____

24. $\frac{4}{5}$ _____

25. $\frac{9}{7}$ _____

26. $\frac{5}{30}$ _____

27. $\frac{16}{32}$ _____

28. $\frac{42}{8}$ _____

29. $\frac{3}{27}$ _____

Name: _____

Date: _____

Section Review ② Covering Sections 1 Through 13

For the following fraction pairs, use <, >, or = to correctly complete the expression.

30. $\frac{1}{3}$ _____ $\frac{5}{9}$

31. $\frac{12}{4}$ _____ $\frac{13}{5}$

32. $\frac{6}{8}$ _____ $\frac{7}{12}$

33. $\frac{6}{7}$ _____ $\frac{4}{9}$

34. $\frac{9}{18}$ _____ $\frac{12}{24}$

35. $\frac{22}{50}$ _____ $\frac{20}{25}$

Add or subtract as indicated. All answers should be in reduced form.

36. $\frac{14}{2} - \frac{2}{5} =$ _____

37. $\frac{4}{8} - \frac{3}{15} =$ _____

38. $1\frac{1}{3} - \frac{7}{9} =$ _____

39. $2\frac{1}{9} + \frac{11}{9} =$ _____

40. $2 + \frac{1}{2} =$ _____

41. $5\frac{1}{5} - \frac{8}{10} =$ _____

42. $2\frac{3}{15} + 1\frac{12}{35} =$ _____

43. $\frac{14}{4} + \frac{6}{3} =$ _____

44. $3\frac{9}{15} + 1\frac{7}{10} =$ _____

45. $\frac{22}{25} - \frac{3}{5} =$ _____

46. $7\frac{1}{4} - 3\frac{2}{5} =$ _____

47. $\frac{3}{10} + \frac{6}{5} + \frac{2}{3} =$ _____

48. $1\frac{1}{2} + \frac{4}{7} + 2\frac{1}{4} =$ _____

Name: _____   Date: _____

Section **14** Converting Decimals to Fractions

ABSORB

In previous sections, we converted fractions to decimals and used those conversions to compare the relative sizes of fractions. It makes sense that decimals should be able to be converted into fractions as well. Here's how the process works:

Example 1:   We'll begin with the decimal number 0.12.

This actually equates to $\frac{12}{100}$ using the place value of decimal numbers, since 0.12 reads as "twelve hundredths."

$\frac{12}{100}$ will reduce to $\frac{3}{25}$, since 4 is a factor of both 12 and 100.

So, $0.12 = \frac{3}{25}$.

Example 2:   Convert 0.34 to a fraction.

$\frac{34}{100}$ reduces to $\frac{17}{50}$.

Example 3:   Convert 2.50 to an equivalent mixed number.

2.50 becomes $2\frac{50}{100}$, which reduces to $2\frac{1}{2}$.

APPLY

Convert the decimals to fractions written in lowest terms. Some may be mixed numbers.

1.   0.22 = _____

2.   0.18 = _____

3.   0.45 = _____

4.   0.25 = _____

5.   0.444 = _____

6.   0.325 = _____

7.   0.825 = _____

8.   10.80 = _____

9.   0.10 = _____

10.   2.75 = _____

11.   0.16 = _____

12.   4.25 = _____

Name: _____ Date: _____

Section **14** Converting Decimals to Fractions

EXTRA PRACTICE   Convert the decimals to fractions written in lowest terms. Some may be mixed numbers.

1. 0.33 = _____

2. 0.15 = _____

3. 0.5 = _____

4. 0.35 = _____

5. 0.555 = _____

6. 0.225 = _____

7. 0.925 = _____

8. 10.90 = _____

9. 0.20 = _____

10. 2.25 = _____

11. 0.17 = _____

12. 4.5 = _____

13. 6.05 = _____

14. 11.13 = _____

15. 2.304 = _____

16. 0.8 = _____

17. 25.256 = _____

18. 0.670 = _____

19. 0.8055 = _____

20. 5.1724 = _____

21. 6.2 = _____

22. 0.009 = _____

23. 0.14 = _____

24. 10.0001 = _____

25. 15.25 = _____

Name: _____ Date: _____

Section 15 Converting Fractions to Percents

ABSORB

Since decimal numbers may easily be converted to percents, fractions may also be converted to percents. The first step is finding the decimal equivalent of the fraction, as we did in previous sections. Then the decimal is converted to a percent.

Example 1: Convert $\frac{4}{10}$ to a percent.

$$\frac{4}{10} = 4 \div 10 = 0.40$$

0.40 then changes to 40% by moving the decimal point two places to the right and adding the % sign.

Example 2: Convert $\frac{5}{8}$ to a percent.

$$\frac{5}{8} = 5 \div 8 = 0.625$$

0.625 becomes 62.5%

Example 3: Convert $3\frac{1}{2}$ to a percent.

$$3\frac{1}{2} = 3 + (1 \div 2) = 3.50$$

3.50 = 350%

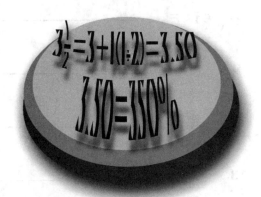

APPLY

Convert the fractions to equivalent percents. (You may stop at two places past the decimal in expressing the percent, i.e., 33.33%. Round the number, if necessary.)

1. $\frac{3}{4} =$ _____

2. $\frac{9}{16} =$ _____

3. $\frac{12}{20} =$ _____

4. $\frac{2}{5} =$ _____

5. $\frac{2}{3} =$ _____

6. $\frac{5}{10} =$ _____

7. $\frac{2}{14} =$ _____

8. $1\frac{4}{5} =$ _____

9. $\frac{1}{8} =$ _____

10. $2\frac{1}{2} =$ _____

11. $\frac{38}{100} =$ _____

12. $\frac{24}{10} =$ _____

Name: _____ Date: _____

Section (15) Converting Fractions to Percents

EXTRA PRACTICE   Convert the fractions to equivalent percents. (You may stop at two places past the decimal in expressing the percent, i.e., 33.33%. Round the number, if necessary.)

1. $\frac{3}{5}$ = _____

2. $\frac{9}{15}$ = _____

3. $\frac{12}{25}$ = _____

4. $\frac{1}{3}$ = _____

5. $\frac{2}{10}$ = _____

6. $\frac{5}{9}$ = _____

7. $\frac{2}{13}$ = _____

8. $1\frac{4}{6}$ = _____

9. $\frac{1}{7}$ = _____

10. $2\frac{1}{4}$ = _____

11. $\frac{38}{99}$ = _____

12. $\frac{25}{12}$ = _____

13. $5\frac{4}{7}$ = _____

14. $\frac{6}{18}$ = _____

15. $\frac{29}{50}$ = _____

16. $\frac{45}{85}$ = _____

17. $3\frac{7}{10}$ = _____

18. $2\frac{11}{24}$ = _____

19. $1\frac{6}{100}$ = _____

20. $\frac{18}{72}$ = _____

21. $\frac{4}{13}$ = _____

22. $4\frac{95}{100}$ = _____

23. $\frac{2}{40}$ = _____

24. $\frac{87}{100}$ = _____

25. $1\frac{9}{65}$ = _____

Name: _____   Date: _____

Section **16** Multiplying Fractions

ABSORB   Here's where the work with fractions actually begins to get easier. There is no need to first get a common denominator before multiplying fractions. The numerator is multiplied by the numerator; likewise, the denominator is multiplied by the denominator.

One thing to keep in mind before multiplying fractions: it will make the problem simpler to reduce the fractions involved before multiplying. So the first step in multiplying fractions is reducing, if the fractions are not already in lowest terms.

Example 1: $\frac{4}{6} \times \frac{1}{9} =$ _____

$\frac{2}{3} \times \frac{1}{9} =$ _____

$\frac{2}{3} \times \frac{1}{9} = \frac{2}{27}$

Example 2: $\frac{5}{6} \times \frac{3}{12} =$ _____

$\frac{5}{6} \times \frac{1}{4} =$ _____

$\frac{5}{6} \times \frac{1}{4} = \frac{5}{24}$

APPLY   Multiply the fractions. Reduce each answer to lowest terms.

1. $\frac{2}{3} \times \frac{4}{5} =$ _____

2. $\frac{3}{8} \times \frac{2}{7} =$ _____

3. $\frac{1}{10} \times \frac{2}{5} =$ _____

4. $\frac{7}{8} \times \frac{3}{12} =$ _____

5. $\frac{1}{2} \times \frac{1}{8} =$ _____

6. $\frac{8}{12} \times \frac{1}{6} =$ _____

7. $\frac{4}{7} \times \frac{8}{16} =$ _____

8. $\frac{2}{5} \times \frac{2}{5} =$ _____

9. $\frac{1}{8} \times \frac{2}{12} =$ _____

10. $\frac{6}{15} \times \frac{4}{6} =$ _____

Name: _____ Date: _____

Section **16** Multiplying Fractions

EXTRA PRACTICE Multiply the fractions. Reduce each answer to lowest terms.

1. $\frac{2}{5} \times \frac{4}{6} =$ _____

2. $\frac{3}{9} \times \frac{2}{5} =$ _____

3. $\frac{1}{12} \times \frac{2}{3} =$ _____

4. $\frac{7}{9} \times \frac{3}{15} =$ _____

5. $\frac{1}{3} \times \frac{1}{7} =$ _____

6. $\frac{8}{15} \times \frac{1}{5} =$ _____

7. $\frac{4}{5} \times \frac{8}{12} =$ _____

8. $\frac{2}{3} \times \frac{2}{3} =$ _____

9. $\frac{1}{7} \times \frac{2}{10} =$ _____

10. $\frac{6}{14} \times \frac{4}{5} =$ _____

11. $\frac{2}{3} \times \frac{6}{9} =$ _____

12. $\frac{3}{24} \times \frac{6}{7} =$ _____

13. $\frac{2}{14} \times \frac{1}{5} =$ _____

14. $\frac{3}{10} \times \frac{12}{18} =$ _____

15. $\frac{13}{26} \times \frac{9}{18} =$ _____

16. $\frac{1}{4} \times \frac{7}{8} =$ _____

17. $\frac{6}{25} \times \frac{4}{12} =$ _____

18. $\frac{5}{8} \times \frac{4}{9} =$ _____

19. $\frac{16}{30} \times \frac{3}{4} =$ _____

20. $\frac{2}{7} \times \frac{10}{25} =$ _____

Name: _____ Date: _____

Section **17** Dividing Fractions

ABSORB The process for dividing fractions is similar to that of multiplying fractions. As with multiplying, it will make the problem easier if fractions are put into fully reduced form before beginning.

The main difference in dividing fracitons is inverting. **Inverting** is the process of flipping the second fraction in order that the division can be performed. (This step actually turns the division problem into a multiplication problem, as we'll see in the examples below.)

Example 1: $\frac{3}{8} \div \frac{1}{2} =$ _____

Invert step: $\frac{3}{8} \times \frac{2}{1} =$ _____

(Only the second fraction is inverted.)

$\frac{3}{8} \times \frac{2}{1} = \frac{6}{8}$

reduces to: $\frac{3}{4}$

Example 2: $\frac{5}{7} \div \frac{1}{3} =$ _____

Invert step: $\frac{5}{7} \times \frac{3}{1} =$ _____

$\frac{5}{7} \times \frac{3}{1} = \frac{15}{7}$

reduces to: $2\frac{1}{7}$

APPLY Divide the fractions. Reduce each answer to lowest terms.

1. $\frac{4}{8} \div \frac{2}{3} =$ _____

2. $\frac{1}{6} \div \frac{1}{9} =$ _____

3. $\frac{5}{6} \div \frac{1}{3} =$ _____

4. $\frac{2}{5} \div \frac{4}{7} =$ _____

5. $\frac{4}{9} \div \frac{1}{5} =$ _____

6. $\frac{2}{9} \div \frac{4}{6} =$ _____

7. $\frac{1}{2} \div \frac{1}{2} =$ _____

8. $\frac{3}{5} \div \frac{2}{3} =$ _____

9. $\frac{1}{7} \div \frac{2}{3} =$ _____

10. $\frac{9}{10} \div \frac{1}{3} =$ _____

Name: _____ Date: _____

Section **17** **Dividing Fractions**

EXTRA PRACTICE   Divide the fractions. Reduce each answer to lowest terms.

1. $\frac{4}{9} \div \frac{2}{5} =$ _____

2. $\frac{1}{5} \div \frac{1}{8} =$ _____

3. $\frac{5}{7} \div \frac{1}{4} =$ _____

4. $\frac{2}{4} \div \frac{4}{8} =$ _____

5. $\frac{4}{8} \div \frac{1}{4} =$ _____

6. $\frac{2}{8} \div \frac{4}{5} =$ _____

7. $\frac{1}{3} \div \frac{1}{3} =$ _____

8. $\frac{3}{4} \div \frac{2}{4} =$ _____

9. $\frac{1}{8} \div \frac{2}{4} =$ _____

10. $\frac{9}{11} \div \frac{1}{4} =$ _____

11. $\frac{12}{15} \div \frac{1}{3} =$ _____

12. $\frac{7}{9} \div \frac{3}{4} =$ _____

13. $\frac{6}{10} \div \frac{4}{12} =$ _____

14. $\frac{5}{7} \div \frac{1}{2} =$ _____

15. $\frac{22}{36} \div \frac{2}{6} =$ _____

16. $\frac{2}{12} \div \frac{4}{5} =$ _____

17. $\frac{6}{8} \div \frac{3}{24} =$ _____

18. $\frac{9}{10} \div \frac{9}{10} =$ _____

19. $\frac{15}{18} \div \frac{4}{9} =$ _____

20. $\frac{1}{2} \div \frac{1}{4} =$ _____

Section 18 Multiplying Fractions and Mixed Numbers

ABSORB

We learned in a previous section how to multiply basic fractions. Problems involving mixed numbers are much the same. The main difference is that a mixed number must first be converted to an improper fraction, and a whole number must likewise be converted to its fractional equivalent.

Keep in mind that reducing fractions before multiplying will keep numbers smaller and make computation easier. Let's also take a quick look at reducing common factors in the overall problem as a way to simplify the multiplication process. You've probably seen this process, sometimes called **cancellation,** before.

Example 1:   (basic variety)

$$2\frac{1}{5} \times \frac{1}{2} = \underline{\hspace{1.5cm}}$$

$$\frac{11}{5} \times \frac{1}{2} = \underline{\hspace{1.5cm}}$$

$$\frac{11}{5} \times \frac{1}{2} = \frac{11}{10}$$

reduces to: $1\frac{1}{10}$

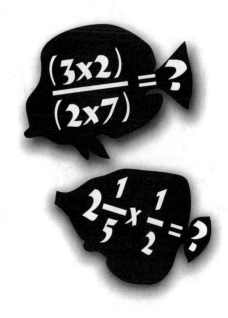

Example 2:   (reducing common factors)

$$1\frac{1}{2} \times \frac{2}{7} = \underline{\hspace{1.5cm}}$$

$$\frac{3}{2} \times \frac{2}{7} = \underline{\hspace{1.5cm}}$$

If we take a moment to examine this problem, it could be rewritten as:

$$\frac{(3 \times 2)}{(2 \times 7)} = \underline{\hspace{1.5cm}}$$

In this problem, 2 is a common factor in both the numerator and the denominator and can therefore be reduced at this stage by "canceling." It's the same as saying $\frac{2}{2} \times \frac{3}{7}$, which will end up being $\frac{3}{7}$ in simplified form. That's because $\frac{2}{2} = 1$, and multiplying something by 1 does not change it.

Name: _____ Date: _____

Section 18 Multiplying Fractions and Mixed Numbers

Example 3: $2\frac{1}{3} \times 1\frac{1}{2} = $ _____

$$\frac{7}{3} \times \frac{3}{2} = $$ _____

Recognizing 3 as a common factor allows this problem to be solved by inspection. The answer is $\frac{7}{2}$, which reduces to $3\frac{1}{2}$. If we continued working the problem without removing the common factor, it would simply end like this:

$$\frac{7}{3} \times \frac{3}{2} = \frac{21}{6} = 3\frac{3}{6} = 3\frac{1}{2}$$

APPLY   Multiply. Reduce common factors when possible to make computations easier. Reduce each answer to lowest terms.

1. $\frac{1}{6} \times \frac{2}{7} = $ _____

2. $\frac{1}{2} \times 2\frac{1}{2} = $ _____

3. $\frac{2}{3} \times 7\frac{1}{2} = $ _____

4. $1\frac{5}{9} \times 2\frac{3}{12} = $ _____

5. $\frac{5}{6} \times 2\frac{1}{8} = $ _____

6. $7\frac{1}{2} \times 2\frac{2}{13} = $ _____

7. $5 \times \frac{4}{4} = $ _____

8. $2\frac{1}{8} \times \frac{16}{34} = $ _____

9. $\frac{3}{18} \times \frac{3}{24} = $ _____

10. $\frac{10}{40} \times \frac{12}{32} = $ _____

11. $\frac{14}{18} \times 3\frac{1}{5} = $ _____

12. $\frac{12}{25} \times \frac{5}{6} = $ _____

13. $1\frac{8}{14} \times 2\frac{1}{3} = $ _____

14. $16 \times \frac{30}{32} = $ _____

54

Name: _____ Date: _____

EXTRA PRACTICE   Multiply. Reduce common factors when possible to make computations easier. Reduce each answer to lowest terms.

1. $\frac{1}{5} \times \frac{2}{8}$ = _____

2. $\frac{1}{3} \times 2\frac{1}{3}$ = _____

3. $\frac{2}{4} \times 7\frac{1}{3}$ = _____

4. $1\frac{5}{8} \times 2\frac{3}{13}$ = _____

5. $\frac{5}{7} \times 2\frac{1}{9}$ = _____

6. $7\frac{1}{3} \times 2\frac{2}{15}$ = _____

7. $10 \times \frac{3}{3}$ = _____

8. $2\frac{1}{9} \times \frac{16}{33}$ = _____

9. $\frac{3}{19} \times \frac{3}{25}$ = _____

10. $\frac{10}{30} \times \frac{12}{33}$ = _____

11. $\frac{14}{19} \times 3\frac{1}{4}$ = _____

12. $\frac{12}{24} \times \frac{5}{7}$ = _____

13. $1\frac{8}{15} \times 2\frac{1}{4}$ = _____

14. $16 \times \frac{30}{33}$ = _____

15. $6\frac{2}{3} \times 2\frac{1}{8}$ = _____

16. $\frac{7}{10} \times 3\frac{11}{12}$ = _____

17. $\frac{8}{8} \times 4\frac{2}{7}$ = _____

18. $9 \times 2\frac{6}{14}$ = _____

19. $1\frac{3}{16} \times 1\frac{5}{7}$ = _____

20. $2\frac{12}{20} \times \frac{3}{4}$ = _____

Section 19 Dividing Fractions and Mixed Numbers

ABSORB

We learned in previous sections how to divide basic fractions. Problems involving mixed numbers are much the same. The main difference is that a mixed number must first be converted to an improper fraction, and a whole number must likewise be converted to its fractional equivalent.

Keep in mind that inverting the second number is still required for division, which effectively turns the problem into a multiplication problem. Also, look for opportunities to reduce fractions or remove common factors to make the computations easier.

Example 1: $\frac{4}{5} \div \frac{2}{3} =$ _____

$\frac{4}{5} \times \frac{3}{2} =$ _____

$\frac{2}{5} \times \frac{3}{1} =$ _____   (remove common factor 2)

$\frac{2}{5} \times \frac{3}{1} = \frac{6}{5}$

reduces to: $1\frac{1}{5}$

Example 2: $2\frac{3}{4} \div \frac{11}{20} =$ _____

$\frac{11}{4} \times \frac{20}{11} =$ _____

$\frac{1}{1} \times \frac{5}{1} =$ _____   (removed common factors 11 and 4)

$\frac{1}{1} \times \frac{5}{1} = \frac{5}{1}$

reduces to: 5

Example 3: $4 \div \frac{6}{7} =$ _____

$\frac{4}{1} \div \frac{6}{7} =$ _____

$\frac{4}{1} \times \frac{7}{6} =$ _____

$\frac{2}{1} \times \frac{7}{3} =$ _____   (removed common factor 2)

$\frac{2}{1} \times \frac{7}{3} = \frac{14}{3}$

reduces to: $4\frac{2}{3}$

Name: _____   Date: _____

Section ⑲ Dividing Fractions and Mixed Numbers

APPLY   Divide. Reduce fractions or remove common factors when possible to make computations easier. Reduce each answer to lowest terms.

1. $\frac{4}{5} \div \frac{7}{9} =$ _____

2. $\frac{7}{10} \div \frac{3}{4} =$ _____

3. $\frac{1}{5} \div \frac{14}{15} =$ _____

4. $4 \div \frac{4}{5} =$ _____

5. $1\frac{1}{2} \div 2\frac{1}{8} =$ _____

6. $\frac{16}{18} \div \frac{3}{24} =$ _____

7. $\frac{13}{27} \div 1 =$ _____

8. $\frac{5}{6} \div 12 =$ _____

9. $\frac{40}{60} \div \frac{10}{20} =$ _____

10. $120 \div \frac{1}{40} =$ _____

11. $\frac{30}{4} \div \frac{20}{3} =$ _____

12. $16 \div \frac{1}{8} =$ _____

13. $\frac{12}{40} \div \frac{1}{4} =$ _____

14. $2\frac{6}{7} \div 1\frac{6}{8} =$ _____

Name: _____ Date: _____

Section 19 Dividing Fractions and Mixed Numbers

EXTRA PRACTICE Divide. Reduce fractions or remove common factors when possible to make computations easier. Reduce each answer to lowest terms.

1. $3\frac{4}{6} \div 1\frac{7}{8} =$ _____

2. $\frac{7}{11} \div \frac{3}{5} =$ _____

3. $5\frac{1}{4} \div 2\frac{14}{16} =$ _____

4. $4 \div \frac{4}{6} =$ _____

5. $1\frac{1}{3} \div 2\frac{1}{9} =$ _____

6. $1\frac{16}{19} \div \frac{3}{25} =$ _____

7. $\frac{13}{25} \div 1 =$ _____

8. $\frac{5}{8} \div 12 =$ _____

9. $\frac{40}{50} \div \frac{10}{30} =$ _____

10. $80 \div \frac{1}{20} =$ _____

11. $\frac{30}{5} \div \frac{20}{4} =$ _____

12. $16 \div \frac{1}{9} =$ _____

13. $\frac{12}{50} \div \frac{1}{5} =$ _____

14. $6\frac{3}{8} \div 3\frac{1}{4} =$ _____

Name: _____ Date: _____

Section **20** More Practice Multiplying and Dividing Fractions

APPLY Multiply or divide as indicated. Reduce each answer to lowest terms.

1. $\frac{3}{13} \times \frac{2}{3} =$ _____

2. $5\frac{5}{8} \times 2 =$ _____

3. $2\frac{3}{16} \times \frac{1}{2} =$ _____

4. $\frac{1}{4} \div 6 =$ _____

5. $100 \div \frac{1}{4} =$ _____

6. $\frac{60}{3} \times 2\frac{2}{3} =$ _____

7. $\frac{3}{4} \div 10 =$ _____

Solve the problems below involving the multiplication and division of fractions. Reduce each answer to lowest terms.

8. If an average milk cow can give $4\frac{2}{3}$ gallons of milk per day, how much milk should a herd of 40 cows produce?

    _____

9. A landowner with 2,100 acres of land split this property equally among 6 children. How much land did each child receive?

    _____

10. If 3 horses eat a total of $\frac{7}{8}$ of a bale of hay per day, how much hay will be needed for the horses for 10 days?

    _____

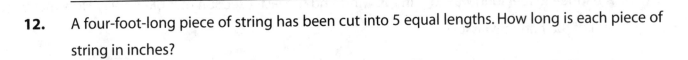

11. Josh makes $\frac{2}{3}$ of the amount of Sheila's salary. How much does Josh make if Sheila's salary is $40,000?

    _____

12. A four-foot-long piece of string has been cut into 5 equal lengths. How long is each piece of string in inches?

    _____

13. A car's gas tank will hold 24 gallons when full. The car's tank is presently $\frac{1}{3}$ full. How much more gas will it take to fill the tank?

    _____

Name: _____

Date: _____

Section 20

Section 20 More Practice Multiplying and Dividing Fractions

14. Steak is priced at $7.50 a pound at Smith's Corner Deli. What would be the charge for a steak that weighs $1\frac{1}{8}$ pounds?

_____

15. Dale bought $10\frac{4}{5}$ gallons of gasoline at a cost of $2.90 per gallon. How much was his total purchase?

_____

16. There are four 50-gallon water tanks at a farm. Each tank has had $\frac{4}{5}$ of the water used. How much water is left in the tanks altogether?

_____

17. In the area where Ethan lives, there has only been $1\frac{1}{2}$ inches of rain over the last 4 months. How many average inches of rain per month have fallen in the last 4 months?

_____

18. A pipe that was originally 16 feet long has had a section $\frac{1}{4}$ of its total length removed. How long was the section of pipe that was removed?

_____

19. A publisher went to press on a group of 5,000 books. It was found that $\frac{3}{4}$ of the books were defective and could not be sold. How many books were not defective?

_____

20. The trout in a hatchery tank all weigh nearly $\frac{4}{5}$ of a pound. It there are 2,000 trout in this tank, about how many pounds of fish is that?

_____

21. A banner 40 feet long was torn in the wind, and the last $\frac{1}{4}$ section of it blew away. How many feet of the banner was lost?

_____

22. A tomato that weighed $3\frac{1}{4}$ pounds won the contest at the fair. How many ounces did it weigh?

_____

Name: _____   Date: _____

Section 20 More Practice Multiplying and Dividing Fractions

EXTRA PRACTICE   Multiply or divide as indicated. Reduce each answer to lowest terms.

1. $\frac{3}{15} \times \frac{2}{5} =$ _____

2. $5\frac{5}{9} \times 2 =$ _____

3. $2\frac{3}{17} \times \frac{1}{3} =$ _____

4. $\frac{1}{5} \div 6 =$ _____

5. $100 \div \frac{1}{5} =$ _____

6. $\frac{60}{4} \times 2\frac{2}{4} =$ _____

7. $\frac{3}{5} \div 10 =$ _____

8. $4\frac{2}{5} \times 40 =$ _____

9. $\frac{7}{9} \times 10 =$ _____

10. $40{,}000 \times \frac{2}{5} =$ _____

11. $24 \times \frac{2}{3} =$ _____

12. $5.5 \times 1\frac{1}{9} =$ _____

13. $10\frac{4}{6} \times 1.8 =$ _____

14. $5\frac{1}{2} \div 0.25 =$ _____

15. $2\frac{6}{7} \div 1\frac{3}{4} =$ _____

16. $9.4 \times \frac{6}{5} =$ _____

17. $14 \div 1\frac{1}{2} =$ _____

18. $3\frac{5}{9} \times 1.6 =$ _____

19. $300 \times \frac{2}{7} =$ _____

20. $20\frac{7}{8} \div 4.5 =$ _____

Name: _____ Date: _____

Section Review ③ Covering Sections 1 Through 20

APPLY Reduce each answer to lowest terms. For improper fractions, write as a mixed number in lowest terms. Write "reduced" for those already in lowest terms.

1. $\frac{23}{40} =$ _____

2. $\frac{44}{12} =$ _____

3. $\frac{1}{15} =$ _____

4. $\frac{21}{41} =$ _____

5. $\frac{7}{4} =$ _____

6. $\frac{125}{15} =$ _____

Convert the fractions to decimal equivalents. Limit your answer to four places past the decimal point, i.e., 1.6667. Round the answer, if necessary.

7. $\frac{50}{75} =$ _____

8. $\frac{2}{26} =$ _____

9. $\frac{85}{5} =$ _____

10. $\frac{8}{106} =$ _____

11. $\frac{4}{9} =$ _____

12. $\frac{20}{210} =$ _____

Use <, >, or = to correctly complete the expression.

13. $\frac{3}{23}$ ____ $\frac{33}{5}$

14. $\frac{1000}{25}$ ____ 25

15. $\frac{12}{5}$ ____ $\frac{5}{12}$

16. $\frac{3}{8}$ ____ $\frac{13}{38}$

17. 18 ____ $\frac{180}{18}$

18. $\frac{5}{12}$ ____ $\frac{4}{11}$

Add or subtract as indicated. Reduce each answer to lowest terms.

19. $\frac{1}{2} - \frac{1}{12} =$ _____

20. $2 - \frac{4}{7} =$ _____

21. $\frac{1}{4} + \frac{5}{4} =$ _____

22. $4\frac{1}{2} + 2\frac{2}{3} =$ _____

23. $\frac{3}{7} - \frac{3}{14} =$ _____

24. $\frac{40}{9} + 1\frac{1}{3} =$ _____

25. $3\frac{5}{16} - 2\frac{1}{8} =$ _____

26. $12\frac{1}{4} - 2\frac{14}{18} =$ _____

27. $\frac{1}{8} + \frac{5}{36} + \frac{1}{4} =$ _____

28. $1\frac{1}{2} + 2\frac{1}{2} + \frac{7}{8} =$ _____

Name: _____ Date: _____

Section Review ③ Covering Sections 1 Through 20

Convert the decimals to fractions written in lowest terms. Some may be mixed numbers.

29. 0.88 = _____

30. 0.300 = _____

31. 0.45 = _____

32. 2.25 = _____

33. 0.64 = _____

34. 4.750 = _____

Convert the fractions to equivalent percents. (You may stop at two places past the decimal point in expressing the percent, i.e., 33.33%.)

35. $\frac{9}{10}$ = _____

36. $\frac{1}{2}$ = _____

37. $\frac{7}{8}$ = _____

38. $\frac{5}{2}$ = _____

39. $\frac{16}{30}$ = _____

40. $\frac{28}{8}$ = _____

Multiply or divide as indicated. Reduce each answer to lowest terms.

41. $\frac{2}{3}$ x $\frac{3}{4}$ = _____

42. $\frac{9}{12}$ x $1\frac{1}{2}$ = _____

43. $\frac{5}{8}$ ÷ $\frac{1}{4}$ = _____

44. $\frac{4}{14}$ x $\frac{7}{2}$ = _____

45. $3\frac{16}{30}$ x 2 = _____

46. 2 ÷ $\frac{1}{20}$ = _____

47. $16\frac{3}{4}$ ÷ 2 = _____

48. $\frac{40}{6}$ ÷ $\frac{20}{12}$ = _____

49. $\frac{7}{10}$ x $\frac{4}{21}$ = _____

50. $1,000$ ÷ $\frac{1}{4}$ = _____

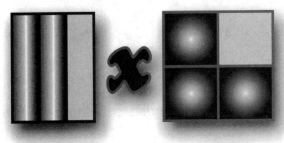

Name: _____ Date: _____

Section Review ③ Covering Sections 1 Through 20

EXTRA PRACTICE   Reduce each answer to lowest terms. For improper fractions, write as a mixed number in lowest terms. Write "reduced" for those already in lowest terms.

1. $\frac{23}{50}$ = _____

2. $\frac{44}{15}$ = _____

3. $\frac{1}{12}$ = _____

4. $\frac{12}{36}$ = _____

5. $\frac{84}{9}$ = _____

6. $\frac{255}{15}$ = _____

Convert the fractions to decimal equivalents. Limit your answer to four places past the decimal point, i.e., 1.6667. Round the answer, if necessary.

7. $\frac{50}{80}$ = _____

8. $\frac{2}{25}$ = _____

9. $\frac{85}{4}$ = _____

10. $\frac{4}{14}$ = _____

11. $\frac{6}{120}$ = _____

12. $\frac{217}{50}$ = _____

Use <, >, or = to correctly complete the expression.

13. $\frac{3}{25}$ _____ $\frac{35}{5}$

14. $\frac{1000}{30}$ _____ 50

15. $\frac{12}{4}$ _____ $\frac{5}{15}$

16. $\frac{7}{15}$ _____ $\frac{8}{19}$

17. $\frac{28}{7}$ _____ $\frac{60}{15}$

18. $\frac{4}{12}$ _____ $\frac{22}{25}$

Add or subtract as indicated. Reduce each answer to lowest terms.

19. $\frac{1}{3} - \frac{1}{15}$ = _____

20. $2 - \frac{4}{8}$ = _____

21. $\frac{1}{5} + \frac{5}{6}$ = _____

22. $4\frac{1}{3} + 2\frac{2}{5}$ = _____

23. $\frac{3}{8} - \frac{3}{15}$ = _____

24. $6\frac{9}{10} + 2\frac{4}{15}$ = _____

25. $\frac{52}{4} - 2\frac{3}{8}$ = _____

26. $20\frac{3}{4} - 5\frac{7}{9}$ = _____

27. $\frac{1}{6} + \frac{7}{25} + \frac{2}{10}$ = _____

28. $2\frac{3}{8} + 4\frac{3}{6} + 5\frac{3}{4}$ = _____

Name: _____   Date: _____

Section Review **3** Covering Sections 1 Through 20

Convert the decimals to fractions written in lowest terms. Some may be mixed numbers.

29.   0.99 = _____   **30.**   0.40 = _____

31.   0.55 = _____   **32.**   10.875 = _____

33.   1.05 = _____   **34.**   8.60 = _____

Convert the fractions to equivalent percents. (You may stop at two places past the decimal point in expressing the percent, i.e., 33.33%.)

35. $\frac{8}{10}$ = _____   **36.** $\frac{1}{3}$ = _____

37. $\frac{7}{9}$ = _____   **38.** $\frac{26}{4}$ = _____

39. $\frac{13}{50}$ = _____   **40.** $\frac{72}{20}$ = _____

Multiply or divide as indicated. Reduce each answer to lowest terms.

41. $\frac{2}{5} \times \frac{3}{5}$ = _____

42. $\frac{9}{15} \times 1\frac{1}{3}$ = _____

43. $\frac{5}{9} \div \frac{1}{5}$ = _____

44. $\frac{4}{15} \times \frac{7}{3}$ = _____

45. $3\frac{16}{25} \times 2$ = _____

46. $\frac{12}{16} \div 4$ = _____

47. $2\frac{4}{5} \div \frac{1}{8}$ = _____

48. $\frac{25}{3} \times \frac{6}{9}$ = _____

49. $620 \div \frac{3}{4}$ = _____

50. $\frac{18}{30} \div \frac{1}{6}$ = _____

Name: _____   Date: _____

Final Review   Covering All Sections

APPLY   Circle the word or phrase that best completes each sentence.

1.   In a fraction, the (numerator, denominator) is the bottom number.

2.   Finding a common denominator is a concern when (adding, multiplying) two fractions.

3.   An improper fraction will reduce to a number that is (less than 1, greater than 1).

4.   If the numerator and denominator of a fraction share a common factor greater than 1, then the fraction can be (reduced, inverted).

5.   A fraction (may, may not) be converted to a decimal number.

6.   It (is, is not) possible to determine the relative size of two fractions.

7.   The figure 25% would be represented by the fraction ($\frac{1}{2}$, $\frac{1}{4}$).

Write a fraction for the portion being described. Reduce each answer to lowest terms.

8.   Fourteen of 22 students were absent on the day before the holiday actually began. Express the portion who were absent.

_____

9.   The Spanish Club had 30 members. Write a fraction to describe 18 who wanted to go on a trip to Mexico.

_____

10.   Of the town's 42 firefighters, 16 volunteered for the special rescue team. Express the portion who did not volunteer.

_____

11.   Of the 26 countries that had signed the original treaty, two later withdrew. Express the portion of the countries that withdrew.

_____

Name: _____ Date: _____

Final Review Covering All Sections

Find the next six multiples for each number.

12. 3 _____

13. 9 _____

14. 12 _____

Find the Least Common Multiple (LCM) for each number.

15. 4, 16 _____

16. 5, 12 _____

17. 3, 8 _____

For each pair of fractions, name the Least Common Denominator (LCD) that could be used.

18. $\frac{5}{8}, \frac{2}{7}$ _____

19. $\frac{1}{10}, \frac{3}{100}$ _____

20. $\frac{1}{2}, \frac{1}{16}$ _____

Add or subtract as indicated. Reduce each answer to lowest terms.

21. $\frac{11}{5} - \frac{6}{5} =$ _____

22. $\frac{3}{4} - \frac{1}{16} =$ _____

23. $\frac{5}{9} + \frac{3}{6} =$ _____

24. $2\frac{1}{2} + \frac{15}{16} =$ _____

25. $4 - \frac{21}{24} =$ _____

26. $1\frac{1}{6} - \frac{4}{5} =$ _____

27. $2\frac{7}{8} + \frac{5}{9} + 3\frac{3}{4} =$ _____

List all factors of the following numbers.

28. 16 _____

29. 100 _____

30. 55 _____

Final Review Covering All Sections

Find the Greatest Common Factor (GCF) for each pair of numbers.

31. 10, 60 _____   **32.** 24, 40 _____

33. 27, 45 _____

Reduce each fraction to lowest terms.

34. $\frac{100}{3}$ = _____   **35.** $\frac{32}{64}$ = _____

36. $\frac{12}{20}$ = _____   **37.** $\frac{64}{144}$ = _____

For each fraction given, convert it to a decimal number and write it in the first column. Then, in the second column, write it as an equivalent percent.

	Decimal	**Percent**
38. $\frac{3}{4}$	_____	_____
39. $1\frac{1}{2}$	_____	_____
40. $\frac{4}{5}$	_____	_____
41. $\frac{3}{8}$	_____	_____

Use <, >, or = to correctly complete each expression.

42. $\frac{3}{4}$ _____ $\frac{15}{16}$

43. $\frac{23}{10}$ _____ $2\frac{3}{7}$

44. $\frac{5}{9}$ _____ $\frac{50}{90}$

45. 12 _____ $\frac{12}{12}$

Name: _____   Date: _____

Final Review   Covering All Sections

Multiply or divide as indicated. Reduce each answer to lowest terms.

46. $\frac{1}{8} \times \frac{3}{4} =$ _____

47. $1\frac{5}{6} \times 2\frac{2}{3} =$ _____

48. $3 \div \frac{2}{3} =$ _____

49. $7\frac{1}{2} \div \frac{4}{5} =$ _____

50. $2\frac{7}{10} \times 5 =$ _____

51. $\frac{8}{9} \div 2 =$ _____

52. $\frac{3}{2} \times \frac{1}{16} =$ _____

Short Answer

53.   Describe the role or purpose of fractions in mathematics.

_____

_____

_____

54.   When multiplying or dividing fractions, why is it important to reduce or cancel common factors when possible?

_____

_____

_____

55.   Place value gives us a quick way to judge the size of a decimal number. Describe a quick way to judge the relative size of a fraction.

_____

_____

_____

Name: _____ Date: _____

Final Review   Covering All Sections

EXTRA PRACTICE   Find the next six multiples for each number.

1.   4   _____   **2.**   10   _____

Find the Least Common Multiple (LCM) for each number.

3.   5, 15 _____   **4.**   6, 13 _____   **5.**   9, 12 _____

For each pair of fractions, name the Least Common Denominator (LCD) that could be used.

6. $\frac{5}{9}, \frac{2}{8}$ _____   **7.** $\frac{1}{12}, \frac{4}{200}$ _____   **8.** $\frac{4}{5}, \frac{7}{8}$ _____

Add or subtract as indicated. Reduce each answer to lowest terms.

9. $\frac{11}{4} - \frac{6}{4} =$ _____   **10.** $\frac{3}{5} - \frac{1}{14} =$ _____

11. $\frac{5}{8} + \frac{3}{5} =$ _____   **12.** $2\frac{1}{3} + \frac{15}{17} =$ _____

13. $6\frac{2}{3} - \frac{5}{12} =$ _____   **14.** $1\frac{1}{4} + 3\frac{9}{21} =$ _____

15. $\frac{8}{12} + \frac{5}{6} + \frac{6}{8} =$ _____

List all factors of the following numbers.

16.   15   _____   **17.**   72   _____

Find the Greatest Common Factor (GCF) for each pair of numbers.

18.   10, 50 _____   **19.**   25, 30 _____   **20.**   18, 42 _____

Write a fraction for the portion being described. Reduce each answer to lowest terms.

21.   Of the library's 56 books on jewelry making, 8 have been checked out. Express the portion of books still in the library. _____

22.   Five of the six candidates for mayor attended a debate before the election. Express the portion of candidates who were at the debate. _____

Name: _____ Date: _____

Final Review Covering All Sections

Reduce each fraction to lowest terms.

23. $\frac{100}{4}$ = _____   **24.** $\frac{32}{65}$ = _____   **25.** $\frac{24}{42}$ = _____

26. $\frac{96}{14}$ = _____   **27.** $\frac{32}{86}$ = _____   **28.** $\frac{59}{4}$ = _____

For each fraction given, convert it to a decimal number and write it in the first column. Then, in the second column, write it as an equivalent percent.

	Decimal	**Percent**
29. $\frac{3}{5}$	_____	_____
30. $1\frac{1}{3}$	_____	_____
31. $\frac{6}{8}$	_____	_____
32. $\frac{35}{50}$	_____	_____

Use <, >, or = to correctly complete each expression.

33. $\frac{3}{5}$ _____ $\frac{15}{17}$ **34.** $\frac{23}{9}$ _____ $2\frac{3}{8}$ **35.** $\frac{8}{16}$ _____ $\frac{12}{24}$

Multiply or divide as indicated. Reduce each answer to lowest terms.

36. $\frac{1}{9} \times \frac{3}{5}$ = _____

37. $1\frac{5}{7} \times 2\frac{2}{4}$ = _____

38. $3 \div \frac{2}{4}$ = _____

39. $7\frac{1}{3} \div \frac{4}{6}$ = _____

40. $3\frac{4}{9} \times 4$ = _____

41. $6\frac{11}{15} \div \frac{2}{3}$ = _____

42. $\frac{10}{7} \times \frac{6}{20}$ = _____

Answer Keys

What Is a Fraction?: *Apply (p. 4)*

1. $\frac{4}{6}$ 2. $\frac{6}{9}$ 3. Answers will vary.

Extra Practice (p. 5)

1. $\frac{1}{2}$ 2. $\frac{4}{9}$ 3. Answers will vary.

A Basic Fraction Has Two Parts: *Apply (p. 6–7)*

1. $\frac{3}{12}$ 2. $\frac{7}{16}$ 3. $\frac{2}{7}$ 4. $\frac{81}{405}$ 5. $\frac{367}{500}$

6. $\frac{16}{76}$ 7. $\frac{11}{14}$ 8. $\frac{3}{8}$ 9. $\frac{44}{200}$ 10. $\frac{13}{17}$

Extra Practice (p. 8–9)

1. $\frac{3}{6}$ 2. $\frac{25}{36}$ 3. $\frac{3}{5}$ 4. $\frac{2}{4}$ 5. $\frac{25}{500}$ 6. $\frac{457}{600}$

7. $\frac{89}{150}$ 8. $\frac{20}{25}$ 9. $\frac{15}{35}$ 10. $\frac{277}{300}$ 11. $\frac{6}{25}$ 12. $\frac{24}{62}$

Finding a Common Denominator: *Apply (p. 10–12)*

1. 3, 6, 9, 12, 15, 18, 21, 24, 27, 30   2. 7, 14, 21, 28, 35, 42, 49, 56, 63, 70

3. 10, 20, 30, 40, 50, 60, 70, 80, 90, 100

4. 20   5. 24   6. 21   7. 36

PART 1:   1. 40   2. 10   3. 12   4a. $\frac{4}{6}, \frac{5}{6}$ 5a. $\frac{10}{60}, \frac{12}{60}$

6a. $\frac{4}{24}, \frac{9}{24}$ 7a. $\frac{2}{14}, \frac{8}{14}$ 8a. $\frac{15}{39}, \frac{1}{39}$ 9a. $\frac{4}{16}, \frac{1}{16}$ 10a. $\frac{6}{8}, \frac{7}{8}$

PART 2:   4b. $\frac{9}{6}$ 5b. $\frac{22}{60}$ 6b. $\frac{13}{24}$ 7b. $\frac{10}{14}$ 8b. $\frac{16}{39}$

9b. $\frac{5}{16}$ 10b. $\frac{13}{8}$

Extra Practice (p. 13)

1. 5, 10, 15, 20, 25, 30, 35, 40, 45, 50   2. 9, 18, 27, 36, 45, 54, 63, 72, 81, 90

3. 11, 22, 33, 44, 55, 66, 77, 88, 99, 110   4. 6, 12, 18, 24, 30, 36, 42, 48, 54, 60

5. 15, 30, 45, 60, 75, 90, 105, 120, 135, 150

6. 12   7. 8   8. 6   9. 9   10. 165   11. 30   12. 44

13. 63   14. 30   15. 90   16. 9   17. 55   18. 12   19. 30

20. 30

Extra Practice (p. 14)

1a. $\frac{75}{120}, \frac{104}{120}$ 2a. $\frac{15}{20}, \frac{7}{20}$ 3a. $\frac{26}{65}, \frac{5}{65}$ 4a. $\frac{8}{12}, \frac{9}{12}$ 5a. $\frac{12}{36}, \frac{9}{36}$ 6a. $\frac{5}{35}, \frac{21}{35}$

7a. $\frac{14}{84}, \frac{60}{84}$ 8a. $\frac{20}{40}, \frac{1}{40}$ 9a. $\frac{5}{15}, \frac{1}{15}$ 10a. $\frac{16}{24}, \frac{15}{24}$

1b. $\frac{179}{120}$ 2b. $\frac{22}{20}$ 3b. $\frac{31}{65}$ 4b. $\frac{17}{12}$ 5b. $\frac{21}{36}$

6b. $\frac{26}{35}$ 7b. $\frac{74}{84}$ 8b. $\frac{21}{40}$ 9b. $\frac{6}{15}$ 10b. $\frac{31}{24}$

Adding Fractions: *Apply (p. 15)*

1. $\frac{2}{3}$ 2. $\frac{5}{7}$ 3. $\frac{13}{12}$ 4. $\frac{4}{8}$ 5. $\frac{11}{12}$ 6. $\frac{15}{24}$ 7. $\frac{61}{45}$

8. $\frac{14}{36}$ 9. $\frac{29}{24}$ 10. $\frac{13}{9}$ 11. $\frac{6}{6}$ 12. $\frac{25}{20}$ 13. $\frac{29}{24}$ 14. $\frac{12}{20}$

15. $\frac{10}{12}$ 16. $\frac{32}{30}$

Extra Practice (p. 16)

1. $\frac{2}{4}$ 2. $\frac{6}{7}$ 3. $\frac{14}{15}$ 4. $\frac{7}{8}$ 5. $\frac{11}{15}$ 6. $\frac{59}{105}$ 7. $\frac{62}{45}$

8. $\frac{44}{96}$ **9.** $\frac{7}{8}$ **10.** $\frac{109}{40}$ **11.** $\frac{24}{30}$ **12.** $\frac{38}{12}$ **13.** $\frac{27}{14}$ **14.** $\frac{23}{21}$

15. $\frac{59}{70}$ **16.** $\frac{31}{24}$ **17.** $\frac{53}{36}$ **18.** $\frac{37}{60}$ **19.** $\frac{199}{210}$ **20.** $\frac{82}{60}$

Subtracting Fractions: *Apply (p. 17)*

1. $\frac{1}{5}$ **2.** $\frac{2}{3}$ **3.** $\frac{3}{7}$ **4.** $\frac{6}{39}$ **5.** $\frac{14}{20}$ **6.** $\frac{7}{50}$ **7.** $\frac{8}{24}$

8. $\frac{110}{120}$ **9.** $\frac{5}{16}$ **10.** $\frac{18}{40}$ **11.** $\frac{9}{20}$ **12.** $\frac{17}{81}$ **13.** $\frac{3}{22}$ **14.** $\frac{20}{30}$

15. $\frac{7}{15}$ **16.** $\frac{1}{9}$

Extra Practice (p. 18)

1. $\frac{1}{5}$ **2.** $\frac{4}{3}$ **3.** $\frac{3}{5}$ **4.** $\frac{12}{96}$ **5.** $\frac{30}{60}$ **6.** $\frac{13}{45}$ **7.** $\frac{68}{175}$

8. $\frac{130}{300}$ **9.** $\frac{34}{105}$ **10.** $\frac{19}{30}$ **11.** $\frac{18}{20}$ **12.** $\frac{18}{80}$ **13.** $\frac{3}{20}$ **14.** $\frac{44}{60}$

15. $\frac{7}{12}$ **16.** $\frac{1}{8}$ **17.** $\frac{48}{12}$ **18.** $\frac{75}{76}$ **19.** $\frac{2}{14}$ **20.** $\frac{7}{20}$

Reducing Fractions: *Apply (p. 19)*

1. 1, 2, 3, 6, 9, 18 **2.** 1, 3, 7, 21 **3.** 1, 2, 3, 4, 6, 8, 12, 24

4. 1, 3, 5, 15 **5.** 12 **6.** 16 **7.** 10

8. 8 **9.** 4 **10.** 9

Extra Practice (p. 20)

1. 1, 2, 3, 5, 6, 10, 15, 30 **2.** 1, 2, 3, 4, 6, 8, 9, 12, 18, 24, 36, 72

3. 1, 5, 25 **4.** 1, 2, 3, 4, 6, 8, 12, 16, 24, 48

5. 1, 3, 9, 27, 81 **6.** 12 **7.** 15 **8.** 20 **9.** 1 **10.** 11

11. 14 **12.** 9 **13.** 7 **14.** 15 **15.** 12 **16.** 3 **17.** 8

18. 4 **19.** 5 **20.** 11

More About Reducing Fractions: *Apply (p. 21)*

1. $\frac{3}{5}$ **2.** reduced **3.** $\frac{1}{2}$ **4.** $\frac{1}{3}$ **5.** $\frac{1}{12}$ **6.** $\frac{1}{4}$ **7.** $\frac{1}{5}$

8. $\frac{1}{3}$ **9.** reduced **10.** $\frac{4}{9}$

Extra Practice (p. 22)

1. reduced **2.** $\frac{1}{25}$ **3.** $\frac{1}{5}$ **4.** reduced **5.** $\frac{1}{5}$ **6.** reduced **7.** $\frac{1}{11}$

8. $\frac{3}{5}$ **9.** $\frac{5}{6}$ **10.** $\frac{1}{4}$ **11.** $\frac{1}{2}$ **12.** $\frac{1}{20}$ **13.** $\frac{1}{3}$ **14.** $\frac{1}{5}$

15. $\frac{1}{11}$ **16.** $\frac{1}{3}$ **17.** reduced **18.** $\frac{1}{9}$ **19.** reduced **20.** $\frac{2}{3}$

21. reduced **22.** $\frac{4}{7}$ **23.** reduced **24.** $\frac{1}{6}$ **25.** $\frac{6}{25}$ **26.** reduced **27.** $\frac{1}{12}$

28. $\frac{12}{25}$ **29.** reduced **30.** $\frac{2}{9}$

Improper Fractions: *Apply (p. 23)*

1. $1\frac{2}{3}$ **2.** $3\frac{1}{2}$ **3.** $1\frac{3}{5}$ **4.** 5 **5.** $2\frac{2}{5}$ **6.** $2\frac{5}{8}$ **7.** 2

8. $1\frac{1}{3}$ **9.** 6 **10.** $2\frac{1}{6}$

Extra Practice (p. 24)

1. $1\frac{1}{4}$ **2.** $2\frac{1}{3}$ **3.** 2 **4.** $3\frac{1}{3}$ **5.** 2 **6.** $2\frac{1}{3}$ **7.** $1\frac{1}{3}$

8. 2 **9.** 3 **10.** 13 **11.** $4\frac{1}{2}$ **12.** $4\frac{1}{2}$ **13.** $1\frac{1}{4}$ **14.** $1\frac{5}{16}$

15. 9 **16.** $8\frac{1}{3}$ **17.** $1\frac{4}{25}$ **18.** $4\frac{3}{7}$ **19.** 11 **20.** $6\frac{1}{3}$

Section Review 1: Covering Sections 1 Through 8: *Apply (p. 25–26)*

1. $\frac{5}{6}$ **2.** $\frac{41}{80}$ **3.** $\frac{19}{20}$ **4.** 4, 8, 12, 16, 20, 24, 28, 32

5. 13, 26, 39, 52, 65, 78, 91, 104   **6.** 24   **7.** 40   **8.** 150   **9.** 24

10. 60   **11.** 64   **12.** 1, 2, 3, 4, 6, 9, 12, 18, 36   **13.** 1, 3, 17, 51

14. 1, 2, 4, 5, 10, 20, 25, 50, 100   **15.** 1, 3, 9, 27   **16.** 12   **17.** 16

18. 3   **19.** 4   **20.** 4   **21.** 1   **22.** 1   **23.** 1   **24.** $\frac{3}{4}$

25. $\frac{17}{56}$ **26.** $1\frac{3}{35}$ **27.** $\frac{1}{2}$ **28.** $\frac{1}{2}$ **29.** $\frac{2}{3}$ **30.** $\frac{11}{14}$ **31.** $5\frac{3}{8}$

32. $6\frac{3}{8}$ **33.** $1\frac{7}{18}$ **34.** $\frac{3}{4}$ **35.** $1\frac{11}{24}$

Extra Practice (p. 27)

1. $\frac{1}{8}$ **2.** $\frac{29}{55}$ **3.** 5, 10, 15, 20, 25, 30, 35, 40   **4.** 25   **5.** 90

6. 45   **7.** 150   **8.** 1, 5, 7, 35   **9.** 1, 2, 4, 13, 26, 52   **10.** 13

11. 4   **12.** $\frac{2}{3}$ **13.** $\frac{11}{12}$ **14.** $\frac{4}{7}$ **15.** $\frac{1}{3}$

Converting Fractions to Decimal Numbers: *Apply (p. 28)*

1. 0.5   **2.** 0.4   **3.** 0.3333   **4.** 0.375   **5.** 0.25

6. 0.5556   **7.** 0.2   **8.** 0.8571   **9.** 0.1667   **10.** 0.1818

11. 0.1429   **12.** 0.16   **13.** 0.125   **14.** 0.22   **15.** 0.1111

16. 0.6842

Extra Practice (p. 29)

1. 0.6667   **2.** 0.8   **3.** 0.5   **4.** 0.3333   **5.** 0.375

6. 0.625   **7.** 0.25   **8.** 0.75   **9.** 0.05   **10.** 0.1667

11. 0.7   **12.** 0.2   **13.** 0.1538   **14.** 0.2444   **15.** 0.7

16. 0.8667   **17.** 0.0333   **18.** 0.0476   **19.** 0.5443   **20.** 0.1667

21. 2.6667   **22.** 2.8   **23.** 2   **24.** 2.8333   **25.** 5.25

26. 18   **27.** 21.3333   **28.** 6.75   **29.** 7.1875   **30.** 3.3333

Ordering Fractions: *Apply (p. 30)*

1. >   **2.** >   **3.** >   **4.** =   **5.** >   **6.** >   **7.** <

8. >   **9.** >   **10.** <   **11.** $\frac{1}{2}$, 0.60, $\frac{6}{8}$ **12.** $\frac{9}{7}$, $\frac{12}{5}$, $\frac{8}{3}$

13. 2.99, 3.12, $3\frac{3}{12}$ **14.** $\frac{7}{6}$, $\frac{4}{3}$, 7.1   **15.** correct

16. 0.100, 1.100, 100   **17.** $\frac{111}{11}$, $10\frac{1}{2}$, 11   **18.** $\frac{1}{5}$, $\frac{11}{44}$, $\frac{3}{8}$

Extra Practice (p. 31)

1. <   **2.** <   **3.** <   **4.** <   **5.** <   **6.** >   **7.** <

8. <   **9.** >   **10.** <   **11.** $\frac{1}{3}$, 0.5, $\frac{6}{8}$ **12.** $\frac{12}{9}$, $\frac{9}{6}$, $\frac{8}{5}$

13. 2.88, $3\frac{3}{15}$, 3.25   **14.** $\frac{7}{5}$, $\frac{4}{2}$, 7.2   **15.** $\frac{6}{4}$, $\frac{9}{4}$, $\frac{5}{2}$ **16.** 0.22, 2.200, 200

17. $\frac{122}{22}$, 12, $12\frac{2}{3}$ **18.** $\frac{1}{4}$, $\frac{3}{9}$, $\frac{11}{22}$ **19.** 0.85, $\frac{7}{8}$, $1\frac{2}{3}$ **20.** $\frac{50}{10}$, 5.1, $5\frac{3}{10}$

Adding Mixed Numbers and Improper Fractions: *Apply (p. 33)*

1. $2\frac{3}{5}$ **2.** $5\frac{5}{12}$ **3.** $5\frac{3}{4}$ **4.** $7\frac{1}{6}$ **5.** $6\frac{2}{5}$ **6.** $42\frac{5}{12}$ **7.** 43

8. $4\frac{3}{10}$ **9.** $4\frac{3}{7}$ **10.** $7\frac{17}{20}$ **11.** $16\frac{1}{3}$ **12.** 1   **13.** $8\frac{1}{8}$ **14.** $5\frac{25}{44}$

15. $6\frac{39}{88}$

Extra Practice (p. 34)

1. $2\frac{11}{12}$ 2. $4\frac{1}{10}$ 3. $6\frac{11}{15}$ 4. $8\frac{2}{15}$ 5. $8\frac{7}{62}$ 6. $32\frac{2}{5}$ 7. $43\frac{7}{45}$
8. $2\frac{13}{15}$ 9. $4\frac{1}{4}$ 10. $7\frac{3}{10}$ 11. $10\frac{1}{3}$ 12. $\frac{167}{220}$ 13. $8\frac{34}{75}$ 14. $5\frac{49}{180}$
15. $5\frac{35}{36}$

Subtracting Mixed Numbers and Improper Fractions: Apply (p. 36)

1. $\frac{5}{8}$ 2. $\frac{7}{9}$ 3. $8\frac{13}{42}$ 4. $1\frac{1}{3}$ 5. $17\frac{23}{60}$ 6. $15\frac{3}{8}$ 7. $2\frac{7}{8}$
8. $1\frac{23}{72}$ 9. $1\frac{17}{32}$ 10. $3\frac{3}{8}$ 11. $4\frac{1}{4}$ 12. $2\frac{1}{10}$ 13. 81 14. $15\frac{1}{12}$
15. $1\frac{19}{30}$

Extra Practice (p. 37)

1. $\frac{22}{45}$ 2. $\frac{3}{4}$ 3. $8\frac{13}{24}$ 4. $1\frac{3}{5}$ 5. $17\frac{3}{5}$ 6. $15\frac{2}{9}$ 7. $1\frac{7}{9}$
8. $1\frac{11}{72}$ 9. $1\frac{331}{595}$ 10. $3\frac{16}{45}$ 11. $3\frac{2}{5}$ 12. $7\frac{73}{100}$ 13. $66\frac{1}{2}$ 14. $15\frac{7}{10}$
15. $\frac{11}{15}$

More Practice Adding and Subtracting Fractions: Apply (p. 38–39)

1. $4\frac{5}{16}$ 2. $3\frac{33}{56}$ 3. $\frac{1}{4}$ 4. $\frac{19}{30}$ 5. $3\frac{1}{3}$ 6. $3\frac{1}{8}$ 7. $\frac{5}{6}$
8. $\frac{11}{15}$ 9. $13\frac{3}{4}$ 10. $13\frac{11}{24}$ 11. $\frac{29}{55}$ 12. $13\frac{20}{21}$ 13. $13\frac{16}{27}$ 14. $8\frac{15}{16}$
15. $9\frac{21}{40}$ 16. $2\frac{25}{72}$ 17. $1\frac{13}{24}$ barrels   18. $\frac{7}{9}$ 19. $\frac{3}{5}$
20. $1\frac{1}{6}$ gallons   21. $\frac{7}{24}$ 22. $\frac{4}{7}$

Extra Practice (p. 40)

1. $3\frac{59}{175}$ 2. $1\frac{13}{20}$ 3. $\frac{7}{12}$ 4. $7\frac{3}{8}$ 5. $3\frac{7}{18}$ 6. $\frac{1}{9}$ 7. $\frac{3}{4}$
8. $\frac{1}{3}$ 9. $1\frac{2}{3}$ bottles   10. $\frac{1}{6}$ skein   11. $\frac{33}{40}$ box   12. $\frac{9}{20}$

Section Review 2: Covering Sections 1 Through 13: Apply (p. 41–42)

1. 12 2. 48 3. 64 4. $1, 2, 11, 22$
5. $1, 2, 3, 4, 6, 8, 12, 16, 24, 48$ 6. $1, 2, 4, 8, 16, 32$ 7. $1, 3, 5, 9, 15, 45$
8. 2 9. 2 10. 12 11. 1 12. 20 13. 7 14. $\frac{2}{3}$
15. $\frac{4}{5}$ 16. $\frac{1}{4}$ 17. $1\frac{2}{3}$ 18. $3\frac{1}{3}$ 19. $\frac{7}{16}$ 20. 0.1875
21. 0.0667 22. 0.375 23. 0.75 24. 0.5714
25. 0.125 26. 1.6667 27. 0.5556 28. 4.0 29. 0.7
30. $<$ 31. $>$ 32. $>$ 33. $>$ 34. $>$ 35. $<$ 36. 4
37. $\frac{5}{18}$ 38. $\frac{5}{8}$ 39. $3\frac{1}{5}$ 40. $3\frac{1}{3}$ 41. $4\frac{13}{36}$ 42. $3\frac{9}{16}$ 43. $1\frac{1}{2}$
44. $7\frac{23}{56}$ 45. $2\frac{4}{7}$ 46. $\frac{37}{60}$ 47. $\frac{41}{72}$ 48. 16

Extra Practice (p. 43–44)

1. 21 2. 30 3. 35 4. $1, 2, 4, 5, 10, 20$ 5. $1, 2, 4, 17, 34, 68$
6. $1, 2, 3, 4, 6, 8, 12, 16, 24, 32, 48, 96$ 7. $1, 2, 3, 4, 6, 9, 12, 18, 36$
8. 5 9. 1 10. 15 11. 2 12. 12 13. 5 14. $\frac{3}{4}$
15. $\frac{2}{3}$ 16. $\frac{1}{5}$ 17. 6 18. $\frac{2}{3}$ 19. $5\frac{4}{5}$ 20. 0.25
21. 0.05 22. 0.3333 23. 0.6667 24. 0.8
25. 1.2857 26. 0.1667 27. 0.5 28. 5.25 29. 0.1111

30. $<$ **31.** $>$ **32.** $>$ **33.** $>$ **34.** $=$ **35.** $<$ **36.** $6\frac{3}{5}$

37. $\frac{3}{10}$ **38.** $\frac{5}{9}$ **39.** $3\frac{1}{3}$ **40.** $2\frac{1}{2}$ **41.** $4\frac{2}{5}$ **42.** $3\frac{19}{35}$ **43.** $5\frac{1}{2}$

44. $5\frac{3}{10}$ **45.** $\frac{7}{25}$ **46.** $3\frac{17}{20}$ **47.** $2\frac{1}{6}$ **48.** $4\frac{9}{28}$

Converting Decimals to Fractions: *Apply (p. 45)*

1. $\frac{11}{50}$ **2.** $\frac{9}{50}$ **3.** $\frac{9}{20}$ **4.** $\frac{1}{4}$ **5.** $\frac{111}{250}$ **6.** $\frac{13}{40}$ **7.** $\frac{33}{40}$

8. $10\frac{4}{5}$ **9.** $\frac{1}{10}$ **10.** $2\frac{3}{4}$ **11.** $\frac{4}{25}$ **12.** $4\frac{1}{4}$

Extra Practice (p. 46)

1. $\frac{33}{100}$ **2.** $\frac{3}{20}$ **3.** $\frac{1}{2}$ **4.** $\frac{7}{20}$ **5.** $\frac{111}{200}$ **6.** $\frac{9}{40}$ **7.** $\frac{37}{40}$

8. $10\frac{9}{10}$ **9.** $\frac{1}{5}$ **10.** $2\frac{1}{4}$ **11.** $\frac{17}{100}$ **12.** $4\frac{1}{2}$ **13.** $6\frac{1}{20}$ **14.** $11\frac{13}{100}$

15. $2\frac{38}{125}$ **16.** $\frac{4}{5}$ **17.** $25\frac{32}{125}$ **18.** $\frac{67}{100}$ **19.** $\frac{1611}{2000}$ **20.** $5\frac{431}{2500}$ **21.** $6\frac{1}{5}$

22. $\frac{9}{1000}$ **23.** $\frac{7}{50}$ **24.** $10\frac{1}{10000}$ **25.** $15\frac{1}{4}$

Converting Fractions to Percents: *Apply (p. 47)*

1. 75% **2.** 56.25% **3.** 60% **4.** 40%

5. 66.67% **6.** 50% **7.** 14.29% **8.** 180%

9. 12.5% **10.** 250% **11.** 38% **12.** 240%

Extra Practice (p. 48)

1. 60% **2.** 60% **3.** 48% **4.** 33.33%

5. 20% **6.** 55.56% **7.** 15.38% **8.** 166.67%

9. 14.29% **10.** 225% **11.** 38.38% **12.** 208.33%

13. 557.14% **14.** 33.33% **15.** 58% **16.** 52.94%

17. 370% **18.** 245.83% **19.** 106% **20.** 25%

21. 30.77% **22.** 495% **23.** 5% **24.** 87% **25.** 113.85%

Multiplying Fractions: *Apply (p. 49)*

1. $\frac{8}{15}$ **2.** $\frac{3}{28}$ **3.** $\frac{1}{25}$ **4.** $\frac{7}{32}$ **5.** $\frac{1}{16}$ **6.** $\frac{1}{9}$ **7.** $\frac{2}{7}$

8. $\frac{4}{25}$ **9.** $\frac{1}{48}$ **10.** $\frac{4}{15}$

Extra Practice (p. 50)

1. $\frac{4}{15}$ **2.** $\frac{2}{15}$ **3.** $\frac{1}{18}$ **4.** $\frac{7}{45}$ **5.** $\frac{1}{21}$ **6.** $\frac{8}{75}$ **7.** $\frac{8}{15}$

8. $\frac{4}{9}$ **9.** $\frac{1}{35}$ **10.** $\frac{12}{35}$ **11.** $\frac{4}{9}$ **12.** $\frac{3}{28}$ **13.** $\frac{1}{35}$ **14.** $\frac{1}{5}$

15. $\frac{1}{4}$ **16.** $\frac{7}{32}$ **17.** $\frac{2}{25}$ **18.** $\frac{5}{18}$ **19.** $\frac{2}{5}$ **20.** $\frac{4}{35}$

Dividing Fractions: *Apply (p. 51)*

1. $\frac{3}{4}$ **2.** $1\frac{1}{2}$ **3.** $2\frac{1}{2}$ **4.** $\frac{7}{10}$ **5.** $2\frac{2}{9}$ **6.** $\frac{1}{3}$ **7.** 1

8. $\frac{9}{10}$ **9.** $\frac{3}{14}$ **10.** $2\frac{7}{10}$

Extra Practice (p. 52)

1. $1\frac{1}{9}$ **2.** $1\frac{3}{5}$ **3.** $2\frac{6}{7}$ **4.** 1 **5.** 2 **6.** $\frac{5}{16}$ **7.** 1

8. $1\frac{1}{2}$ **9.** $\frac{1}{4}$ **10.** $3\frac{3}{11}$ **11.** $2\frac{2}{5}$ **12.** $1\frac{1}{27}$ **13.** $1\frac{4}{5}$ **14.** $1\frac{3}{7}$

15. $1\frac{5}{6}$ **16.** $\frac{5}{24}$ **17.** 6 **18.** 1 **19.** $1\frac{7}{8}$ **20.** 2

Multiplying Fractions and Mixed Numbers: *Apply (p. 54)*

1. $\frac{1}{21}$　2. $1\frac{1}{4}$　3. 5　4. $3\frac{1}{2}$　5. $1\frac{37}{48}$　6. $16\frac{2}{13}$　7. 5
8. 1　9. $\frac{1}{48}$　10. $\frac{3}{32}$　11. $2\frac{22}{45}$　12. $\frac{2}{5}$　13. $3\frac{2}{3}$　14. 15

Extra Practice (p. 55)

1. $\frac{1}{20}$　2. $\frac{7}{9}$　3. $3\frac{2}{3}$　4. $3\frac{5}{8}$　5. $1\frac{32}{63}$　6. $15\frac{29}{45}$　7. 10
8. $1\frac{7}{297}$　9. $\frac{9}{475}$　10. $\frac{4}{33}$　11. $2\frac{15}{38}$　12. $\frac{5}{14}$　13. $3\frac{9}{20}$　14. $14\frac{6}{11}$
15. $14\frac{1}{6}$　16. $2\frac{89}{120}$　17. $4\frac{2}{7}$　18. $21\frac{6}{7}$　19. $2\frac{1}{28}$　20. $1\frac{19}{20}$

Dividing Fractions and Mixed Numbers: *Apply (p. 57)*

1. $1\frac{1}{35}$　2. $\frac{14}{15}$　3. $\frac{3}{14}$　4. 5　5. $\frac{12}{17}$　6. $7\frac{1}{9}$　7. $\frac{13}{27}$
8. $\frac{5}{72}$　9. $1\frac{1}{3}$　10. 4,800　11. $1\frac{1}{8}$　12. 128　13. $1\frac{1}{5}$　14. $1\frac{31}{49}$

Extra Practice (p. 58)

1. $1\frac{43}{45}$　2. $1\frac{2}{33}$　3. $1\frac{19}{23}$　4. 6　5. $\frac{12}{19}$　6. $15\frac{20}{57}$　7. $\frac{13}{25}$
8. $\frac{5}{96}$　9. $2\frac{2}{5}$　10. 1,600　11. $1\frac{1}{5}$　12. 144　13. $1\frac{1}{5}$　14. $1\frac{25}{26}$

More Practice Multiplying and Dividing Fractions: *Apply (p. 59–60)*

1. $\frac{2}{13}$　2. $11\frac{1}{4}$　3. $1\frac{3}{32}$　4. $\frac{1}{24}$　5. 400　6. $53\frac{1}{3}$　7. $\frac{3}{40}$
8. $186\frac{2}{3}$ gallons　9. 350 acres　10. $8\frac{3}{4}$ bales　11. $26,666.67
12. $9\frac{3}{5}$ inches　13. 16 gallons　14. $8.44　15. $31.32
16. 40 gallons　17. $\frac{3}{8}$ inches　18. 4 feet　19. 1,250 books
20. 1,600 pounds　21. 10 feet　22. 52 ounces

Extra Practice (p. 61)

1. $\frac{2}{25}$　2. $11\frac{1}{9}$　3. $\frac{37}{51}$　4. $\frac{1}{30}$　5. 500　6. $37\frac{1}{2}$　7. $\frac{3}{50}$
8. 176　9. $7\frac{7}{9}$　10. 16,000　11. 16　12. $6\frac{1}{9}$　13. $19\frac{1}{5}$　14. 22
15. $1\frac{31}{49}$　16. $11\frac{7}{25}$　17. $9\frac{1}{3}$　18. $5\frac{31}{45}$　19. $85\frac{5}{7}$　20. $4\frac{23}{36}$

Section Review 3: Covering Sections 1 Through 20: *Apply (p. 62–63)*

1. reduced　2. $3\frac{2}{3}$　3. reduced　4. reduced　5. $1\frac{3}{4}$
6. $8\frac{1}{3}$　7. 0.6667　8. 0.0769　9. 17.0　10. 0.0755
11. 0.4444　12. 0.0952　13. <　14. >　15. >
16. >　17. >　18. >　19. $\frac{5}{12}$　20. $1\frac{3}{7}$　21. $1\frac{1}{2}$　22. $7\frac{1}{6}$
23. $\frac{3}{14}$　24. $5\frac{7}{9}$　25. $1\frac{3}{16}$　26. $9\frac{17}{36}$　27. $\frac{37}{72}$　28. $4\frac{7}{8}$　29. $\frac{22}{25}$
30. $\frac{3}{10}$　31. $\frac{9}{20}$　32. $2\frac{1}{4}$　33. $\frac{16}{25}$　34. $4\frac{3}{4}$　35. 90%　36. 50%
37. 87.5%　38. 250%　39. 53.33%　40. 350%　41. $\frac{1}{2}$
42. $1\frac{1}{8}$　43. $2\frac{1}{2}$　44. 1　45. $7\frac{1}{15}$　46. 40　47. $8\frac{3}{8}$　48. 4
49. $\frac{2}{15}$　50. 4,000

Extra Practice (p. 64–65)

1. reduced
2. $2\frac{14}{15}$
3. reduced
4. $\frac{1}{3}$
5. $9\frac{1}{3}$
6. 17
7. 0.625
8. 0.08
9. 21.25
10. 0.2857
11. 0.05
12. 4.34
13. $<$
14. $<$
15. $>$
16. $>$
17. $=$
18. $<$
19. $\frac{4}{15}$
20. $1\frac{1}{2}$
21. $1\frac{1}{30}$
22. $6\frac{11}{15}$
23. $\frac{7}{40}$
24. $9\frac{1}{6}$
25. $10\frac{5}{8}$
26. $14\frac{35}{36}$
27. $\frac{97}{150}$
28. $12\frac{5}{8}$
29. $\frac{99}{100}$
30. $\frac{2}{5}$
31. $\frac{11}{20}$
32. $10\frac{7}{8}$
33. $1\frac{1}{20}$
34. $8\frac{3}{5}$
35. 80%
36. 33.33%
37. 77.78%
38. 650%
39. 26%
40. 360%
41. $\frac{6}{25}$
42. $\frac{4}{5}$
43. $2\frac{7}{9}$
44. $\frac{28}{45}$
45. $7\frac{7}{25}$
46. $\frac{3}{16}$
47. $22\frac{2}{5}$
48. $5\frac{5}{9}$
49. $826\frac{2}{3}$
50. $3\frac{3}{5}$

Final Review: Covering All Sections: Apply (p. 66–69)

1. denominator
2. adding
3. greater than 1
4. reduced
5. may
6. is
7. $\frac{1}{4}$
8. $\frac{7}{11}$
9. $\frac{3}{5}$
10. $\frac{13}{21}$
11. $\frac{1}{13}$
12. 6, 9, 12, 15, 18, 21
13. 18, 27, 36, 45, 54, 63
14. 24, 36, 48, 60, 72, 84
15. 16
16. 60
17. 24
18. 56
19. 100
20. 16
21. 1
22. $\frac{11}{16}$
23. $1\frac{1}{18}$
24. $3\frac{7}{16}$
25. $3\frac{1}{8}$
26. $\frac{11}{30}$
27. $7\frac{13}{72}$
28. 1, 2, 4, 8, 16
29. 1, 2, 4, 5, 10, 20, 25, 50, 100
30. 1, 5, 11, 55
31. 10
32. 8
33. 9
34. $33\frac{1}{3}$
35. $\frac{1}{2}$
36. $\frac{3}{5}$
37. $\frac{4}{9}$
38. 0.75, 75%
39. 1.5, 150%
40. 0.80, 80%
41. 0.375, 37.5%
42. $<$
43. $<$
44. $=$
45. $>$
46. $\frac{3}{32}$
47. $4\frac{8}{9}$
48. $4\frac{1}{2}$
49. $9\frac{3}{8}$
50. $13\frac{1}{2}$
51. $\frac{4}{9}$
52. $\frac{3}{32}$
53. Fractions are used for expressing both portions of a whole and portions of a group.
54. Computations are easier when working with smaller numbers.
55. A quick way to gauge the size of a fraction is to look at how large the numerator is in relation to the denominator.

Extra Practice (p. 70–71)

1. 8, 12, 16, 20, 24, 28
2. 20, 30, 40, 50, 60, 70
3. 15
4. 78
5. 36
6. 72
7. 600
8. 40
9. $1\frac{1}{4}$
10. $\frac{37}{70}$
11. $1\frac{9}{40}$
12. $3\frac{11}{51}$
13. $6\frac{1}{4}$
14. $4\frac{19}{28}$
15. $2\frac{1}{4}$
16. 1, 3, 5, 15
17. 1, 2, 3, 4, 6, 8, 9, 12, 18, 24, 36, 72
18. 10
19. 5
20. 6
21. $\frac{6}{7}$
22. $\frac{5}{6}$
23. 25
24. reduced
25. $\frac{4}{7}$
26. $6\frac{6}{7}$
27. $\frac{16}{43}$
28. $14\frac{3}{4}$
29. 0.6, 60%
30. 1.3333, 133.33%
31. 0.75, 75%
32. 0.7, 70%
33. $<$
34. $>$
35. $=$
36. $\frac{1}{15}$
37. $4\frac{2}{7}$
38. 6
39. 11
40. $13\frac{7}{9}$
41. $10\frac{1}{10}$
42. $\frac{3}{7}$